The **Counter**Cultural South

The Counter Cultural SOUTH

JACK TEMPLE KIRBY

Mercer University Lamar Memorial Lectures No. 38

The University of Georgia Press   Athens & London

Designed by Sandra Strother Hudson

Set in 10 on 14 Baskerville by

Tseng Information Systems, Inc.

Printed and bound by Thomson-Shore

The paper in this book meets the guidelines

for permanence and durability of the Committee on

Production Guidelines for Book Longevity

of the Council on Library Resources.

Printed in the United States of America

99 98 97 96 95 C 5 4 3 2 1

Library of Congress Cataloging in Publication Data

Kirby, Jack Temple.

The countercultural South / Jack Temple Kirby.

p.   cm. — (Mercer University Lamar Memorial
Lectures; no. 38)

Includes bibliographical references and index.

ISBN 0-8203-1723-3 (alk. paper)

1. Southern States—Social conditions—1945–

2. Social classes—Southern States.   3. Southern

States—Race relations.   4. Marginality, Social—

Southern States.   I. Title.   II. Series.

HN79.A13K565   1995

306'.0975—dc20   94-39609

British Library Cataloging in Publication Data available

for
Elizabeth Kirby Andrews

Contents

Foreword

*M*ost of us involved in Mercer University's life today are not from Eugenia Dorothy Blount Lamar's generation; we have lived in what could be called a different world. But it is not difficult for us to appreciate what she did for Mercer University when she left us the endowment that makes the Lamar Memorial Lectures possible.

She said that she wanted the lectures to be of "the very highest type of scholarship" and to "aid in the permanent preservation of the values of southern culture, history, and literature." We think that the Lamar Lectures committees over the last thirty-eight years, including members retired, like Malcolm Lester and Benjamin Griffith, and members deceased, like Spencer King, have upheld the bequest's purpose of presenting scholarship of "the very highest type" as well as anyone could. From scholars nationally, and even internationally, respected we have heard, and read later as University of Georgia Press books, some very worthy scholarship.

Regarding Mrs. Lamar's other stipulation, that the lectures "aid in the permanent preservation of the values of southern culture, history, and literature," perhaps no culture's values are final and permanent. But there is something in southern culture that is magnetic, even as we acknowledge and investigate what is countercultural to it or in it, as Professor Jack Temple Kirby does in the present lectures. There is something in the South that deserves our attention and study, whether it is permanently preservable or not, and Mrs. Lamar's generosity makes this form of that study possible; for that reason, we continue two generations later, and from a much different world, to honor her memory.

In October 1994 Mercer University was fortunate to hear Professor Kirby use the breadth and depth of his scholarship to reflect on the countercultural South. According to Professor Kirby, there have remained alive in the South of the twentieth century at least two groups of people who have been "countercultural" in that they have resisted incorporation into the mainstream of southern culture—southern African Americans and poor southern whites. These lectures explore some of the motivations and the methods of their countercultural presence and conclude by identifying voices in the South who speak for the counterculture or who at least do not speak of it condescendingly or patronizingly.

Professor Kirby was a most genial and witty guest to our campus, and his lectures found one of the most responsive audiences in the history of these lectures. Mrs. Lamar's idea thrives.

> MICHAEL M. CASS
> for the Lamar Memorial Lectures Committee

Acknowledgments

ere it not for the generosity and farsightedness of the late Mrs. Eugenia Dorothy Blount Lamar, there would not be a nearly four-decades-long tradition of exemplary speechifying on southern culture each fall at Mercer University in the lovely city of Macon, Georgia. As an undergraduate, I came to understand that the published Lamar Lectures were an accumulating critical literature of the South not to be ignored. And not much later, I began secretly to hope that some day I might join the succession of distinguished lecturers myself. Realization—the gratifying occupation of Jesse Mercer's own pulpit in the "Sanctuary"—confirms another virtue of the Macon community, its legendary hospitality. *Mi compañera* and I were not only luxuriously lodged and delectably dined but also guided about and introduced with a gracefulness that must have represented the most thorough and thoughtful preparation for our visit.

So our admiration as well as thanks go to the Lamar Committee, especially the engaging Mrs. R. Lanier Anderson III, the courtly Henry Y. Warnock, the faithful Wayne Mixon (who invited me to lecture), and most of all the current committee chair Michael Cass, and also Lynn Stovall Cass. They and other Maconians were better than hosts; they were boon companions.

My own institution, Miami University, was generous to me in preparation of the lectures. This published version emerged from a semester's leave, revisions and the condensed lectures from a summer research appointment. I am grateful as well to colleagues here and abroad who read chapters/lectures and gave me the benefit of their smart perceptions: Andrew R. L.

Cayton, James C. Cobb, Pete Daniel, Mary E. Frederickson, and John Shelton Reed. My boonest companion and muse, La Constancia, read the entirety twice, enlarging again my unredeemable indebtedness to her. Finally, I dedicate this little book to my dear sister, Betsy. For while I meditate upon race and class in the South, secure in my white middle-class northern exile, Betsy has engaged both difficult subjects for decades, in a difficult southern place, with insight and sympathy beyond most mortals.

The CounterCultural South

Introduction

*T*his little volume comprises three chapters that might be read as discrete essays, in any order. The first chapter considers black working folk (especially southern men), their ingenious tradition of negotiating with bosses, and a nonnegotiating tradition that has recently and disturbingly (I suggest) become common among men born just as the civil rights movement was underway in the 1950s. The second chapter assays the persistence of a species of separatism among humble rural white southerners that is called frontierism. The third turns to the sorry public repute of these southern whites, with an elaborate consideration of their habilitation.

On the other hand, I intend collective meaning for the essays as well. The Lamar Memorial Lectures format is appropriately brief, but I ambitiously (and foolheartedly, for certain) address subjects quite encompassing—race and social class, and southerners' resistance to or noncollaboration with the hegemonic national (as well as regional) culture of capitalist individualism. I suggest, in other words, that a not-quite-measurable but substantial minority of southerners are countercultural. Some resist in peaceful and conventional ways, such as labor union activism. Others avoid contact so far as they can, sustaining existence on a shrinking margin of society. That these two behaviors more or less correspond to color—blacks negotiating, whites in flight—renders consideration of the countercultural problematic. Black workers are progressive, historically evolved as it were; whites are not. Yet this paradox might explain why today, three decades after the legislative successes of the civil rights movement, black and white working-class southerners seldom vote together, and why they inform poll-

1

sters of virtually opposite notions of individuals' and governments' roles in establishing economic well-being.

$\mathscr{T}$he bourgeois hegemony in the South is relatively recent. To be sure, the antebellum South was crowded with native white (and a few black) investors, builders, and bankers. Some of these were a part of the culture of work, discipline, efficiency, saving, and capitalist social relations associated with Yankees and western Europeans. The region's important place in a world market system rendered such exceptions inevitable. But exceptional they were. For the antebellum South was primarily a civilization based upon noncapitalist—indeed, anticapitalist—labor and social relations, and its people were shamelessly devoted to leisure and indiscipline, maddeningly indifferent to technology and growth.[1]

The contemporary bourgeoisie's functional and spiritual ancestors are probably best located among the myriad guano salesmen, country store merchants and clerks, railroad agents and various branch-bank operatives who fostered the vast expansion of cotton culture during the last thirty-five years of the nineteenth century. Collectively, they undermined premodern economies of mutual exchange and substituted for them not only the structures of modern exchange but also the beliefs and behaviors commonly associated with bourgeois culture. Meanwhile, southern textile-mill founders and other industrialists introduced corporate capitalism—the larger-scale, bureaucratic counterpart to entrepreneurial capitalism. The process of capitalizing the southern hinterland consumed the efforts of several generations, proceeding over the landscape according to geologic degree of difficulty. Remote parts of Appalachia, for example, were not brought fully into national and world market relations until the fourth, fifth, sixth, and even seventh decades of the twentieth century.[2]

Despite all this, the South remained profoundly different, only precariously a dominion of the bourgeoisie. Most manufacturing enterprises were located apart from cities, and there most remain. Another peculiarity of capitalism in the South is its persisting reliance upon agriculture and the extraction of natural resources. Manufacturing employment in textiles, for instance, did not exceed that in lumber and other wood products until 1930; and overall manufacturing employment did not overtake the region's number of farms until the late 1940s. The latter event illustrates another great fact of southern economic history—the isolation and entrapment of southern workers. They could not move freely into the national labor pool until passage of the Fair Labor Standards Act of 1938, and hardly did so before the unprecedented demands of World War II. Still, half a century after the war's end, workers who remain in the region are paid somewhat less than other Americans (including brothers and sisters who migrated), and southern industries are more likely to be extractive and remote from cities.[3]

Conceding the South's legitimate, even exuberant, place in the dominant national culture, these peculiarities have invited and defined a large countercultural presence. This countercultural South is widely acknowledged and almost totally (perhaps willfully) misrepresented as superficial, curmudgeonly regional male *style:* southerners (read "white middle and upper classes") are archconservative politically, dangerously aggressive in pursuit of violent sport, and excessively familiar in social relations. Southerners (read "rednecks" and "hillbillies") are quaint premoderns, prone to taking the law into their own hands, but entertaining despite their doleful delinquencies of discipline and taste. And southerners (read "the black poor and working class" throughout the country, for all sound southern) are lazy and immoral, our principal criminal population.[4]

The first "style" is of course not countercultural at all. Archconservative in late-twentieth-century political parlance means primarily allegiance to unregulated free-market capitalism. Love of collegiate and professional sports (especially football) is broadly (and properly) perceived as a metaphor for war *and* business competition—violent team play within recognized rules, for the purpose of gain and demonstration of divine grace. And prepossessing friendliness is a hallmark not only of certain tribal cultures but also of the Jaycees. Rather, the second and third characterizations of southernness—that of the working classes and poor of both races—begin to suggest the genuinely countercultural.

The hostility implicit in popular perception of nonconforming white and black working-class and poor southerners signifies not only their marginality to the formal culture but also the subversiveness these classes manifest. The Jaycees and fellow communitarians of bourgeois culture are builders committed to material progress. Their political opposition to "change" notwithstanding, the bourgeoisie are possessed of a linear historical sense that the past is, well, outdated. Modern technology and the discipline of work bring them the money to surround themselves with material signifiers of their legitimacy in historical progression. Those lacking these signifiers—or worse, indifferent to them—are doomed, historically and therefore morally, too. The countercultural classes, meanwhile, in effect discipline the dominant by passively embodying the abyss into which the lax might fall, simultaneously defining (via contrast) the moral justification of the dominant groups. Some active countercultural expression, too—jazz and the blues, black and white, most obviously—also serves bourgeois culture, providing blessed relief from confining proprieties. More generally, however, one must conclude that the United States' upper classes mostly fear the countercultural classes. How else explain the condescension and cruelty of representations of the lower classes of either race?

By the mid-1990s, a vast and subversive "white trash" had nearly eclipsed the "black underclass" as a threat to morality and economic progress. *New York* magazine decried a runaway nationalization of "White-trash behavior . . . defined by childlikeness and the headlong pursuit of easy gratification—quite often, sex." Illegitimacy and illiteracy soared with plastic flamingo sales and the ratings for television's *Roseanne*. Dutiful labor and deferred pleasure had fallen out of fashion, declared *New York's* Jeremiah. "True trash is unsocialized and violent. . . . True trash takes what it needs and claims it's what it deserves." The Republic's worthy and respectable, meanwhile—and the virtues they represent—are in grave peril.[5]

*C*oping with such perception is very problematical. First, social class is my subject, but class is more complex than property- and income-levels, as everyone knows. All those without money are not hostile or indifferent to bourgeois standards and aspirations, either. There is evidence—mostly anecdotal but rather overwhelming, I think—that discipline, striving, and greed are rife among the South's and every other region's and nation's "underprivileged" peoples. Then there is the sorrowfully chasmic divergence of southern whites and blacks, whose countercultural beliefs and behaviors are so different (actually, the opposite in an important sense), that they must be treated separately.

The southern races' persisting differences of opinion are documented all too well in a monograph by the political scientist twins Earl and Merle Black, *Politics and Society in the South* (1987). It was here—and beyond the Black brothers' context—that I first spied evidence of countercultural belief and behavior in the region. The Blacks relentlessly pursued the races' separate political behavior in the post–civil rights movement South, then sought ideological explanations. Certain polling results revealed fundamental value differences. Most interesting to me was a set of polls conducted between 1972 and 1984 that asked respondents who was more responsible for economic well-being, the individual or the government? Among blacks—unfortunately not differentiated by class, but most of whom were apparently working class— 72 percent placed "greater stress on governmental responsibility." A mere thirteen percent thought the individual was responsible. (The remaining fourteen percent waffled at a statistical "midpoint.") White respondents were divided by class. Of the middle class, 56 percent stressed individual responsibility for economic well-being; 49 percent of the white working class agreed. Large proportions of the white middle and working classes waffled on the question—21 and 23 percent, respectively; their ambivalence may be very significant. But the Black brothers' point was well made: there was a stunning divergence between the races, the whites appearing rather "bourgeois" on this key question of policy and personal values, blacks overwhelmingly otherwise.[6]

The political scientists were content, meanwhile, with their demonstration of divergence, here and elsewhere in their fine work. As an historian, however, I wondered about the sources of black southerners' differentness. Were they, as hostile white subjects put it to interviewers, simply cynical recipients of government largess?[7] I suspected not. Black respondents' rejection of the myth of individual responsibility so essential to bourgeois ideology reveals them, to me, as modern folk who understand systems, the power relationships within political economies. Are we to understand black southerners' progressivism, then, as a product of their historical experience as slaves and sharecroppers, as victims of Jim Crow's oppressions? Yes, but I think this not enough. So in the first of the following chapters, I shall explore a theme of blacks' working relationships and their *negotiations* with succeeding forms of adversity as source and demonstration of their progressivism.

The political scientists' data on white opinion on responsibility for economic well-being is more complex. Assuming enormous forces for white solidarity, I was frankly surprised that nearly a third of workers polled (29 percent) declared government, rather than the individual, as captain of society's fate. Added to the 23 percent who waffled, these respondents constituted slightly more than half the total. And, as already observed, even a substantial minority of the white middle class offered objection to the bourgeois myth.[8]

Still, one must not conclude too much from polls. The composition of questions limits responses, as ever, and we have no way of knowing if respondents (whatever their color or class), insisting on individual responsibility for economic well-being, do not simply distrust government as another distant, illogical force afoot in the world, disturbing tranquility. Pollsters too often assume comfort with global language in their subjects. I suspect that working-class whites, especially, were troubled by the choices presented them. (They had the highest "waffle" point of any group surveyed.)

So, in another essay I will attempt a redefinition of lower-class whites' "conservatism" that takes account of their apparent ambivalence. Most of them resist progressivism despite circumstances of life closely corresponding to those of progressive blacks. But must one reason that "conservative" is bourgeois? Clearly, this would be in error. For American individualism is, after all, a faith and behavior older than market and industrial capitalism. I will suggest that lower-class white southerners, too, are creatures of a peculiar past; but unlike black southerners, they have little experience with negotiation.

A last essay is an excursion into the literature (and two other media) about poor southern whites. This has been, in the main, a sorry business. At last, however, I recommend several works of autobiography, fiction, and nonfiction that suggest a further reconfiguration of the traditional southern canon. For rather than reducing a vast and complex countryside and its peoples to a single set of condescending abstractions, these works sympathetically illuminate divergences, paradoxes, and ambiguities in ordinary southerners' lives, embracing without apology the wonderful specificities of place within the mythical realm called the South.

Negotiators/Nonnegotiators ONE

Ever after I entertained the first idea of being free, I had endeavored
so to conduct myself as not to become obnoxious to the white inhabitants,
knowing as I did their power, and their hostility. . . . This all colored people
at the south, free and slaves, find it peculiarly necessary for their own
comfort and safety to observe.
—Lunsford Lane, 1848

What has changed [since the early 1970s]? What went wrong? The bitter
irony of integration . . . The virtual collapse of rising expectations? . . .
I believe that two significant reasons why the threat [of nihilism] is
more powerful now than ever before are the saturation of market forces
and market moralities in black life and the present crisis in black leadership.
—Cornel West, 1993

Stagolee went walkin'
with his .40 gun in his hand;
He said, "I feel mistreated this mornin',
I could kill most any man."
—Folk song, ca. 1895

Nineteen fifty-five was the year of the Montgomery
bus boycott and the emergence of the charismatic Martin
Luther King, Jr.—the conventionally understood origin of the
decade-long civil rights movement, the beginning of the end
of Jim Crow in the American South. The year also lay on the
cusp of the era of rock and roll, the music of countercultural
youth and the solvent, many still declare, that unglued the
social order. Rock and roll was African-American "rhythm
and blues," crossbred and internationalized. An example of its

roots was a commercial version of a black folk song, "Stagger Lee" (as Lloyd Price spelled it), released the year after Montgomery's buses were integrated. (The antiheroic title character has also been known as "Stag O'Lee," "Stagolee," "Stackolee," etc.) The disarmingly light arrangement—like Bobby Darin's near-contemporaneous "Mack the Knife"—could not disguise the terrifying content of the song's lyrics, however. "Stag" was a remorseless killer, scarier than "Mack" because he murdered more publicly, and because he murdered from the context of a particular male code of honor that promised no compromise, no peace, ever. In many versions of "Stagger Lee" (including Price's and John Hurt's), Stag's victim, Billy, had merely disrespected Stag's Stetson hat during a game of cards. Stag leveled his gun, heedless to Billy's pleas for his wife and little children, and blew Billy away. Price's recording played the scene over and over during the same years that other black people, Christian and mostly middle class, promised social and spiritual redemption through nonviolent sacrifice.[1]

*T*he same year that Rosa Parks rebelled on her Montgomery bus, there was born in the South a black baby named Nathan McCall. His first nine years were itinerant—his stepfather was a sailor; McCall lived in Norfolk, in Morocco, then Key West. In 1964, the year of the Civil Rights Act, when Nathan was nine, his family settled in Portsmouth, Virginia, in a new black working-class suburb improbably called Cavalier Manor. Nathan was a smart student, and he helped desegregate a formerly all-white junior high school. Then began a near-fatal downward spiral. Infected, like so many of us males, with what could be called testosterone poisoning, he became a gang member, a fighter, a victimizer of hapless white boys but more often of other blacks, a rapist, a dope dealer, a burglar, and eventually an armed holdup man. One night in an amusement park, in front of scores of witnesses, McCall, still a teenager, shot a fellow in the chest who had disrespected his woman, the mother of his young son. This victim, luckily, survived, and McCall—a Stag O'Lee for the 1970s—got off with a brief jail term. At the age of twenty, however, for pointing (not firing) a gun during a holdup of a white-owned fast-food store in Norfolk, McCall received an eight-year prison sentence. He served three years before being paroled, mostly at the Southampton Correctional Institution.[2] Coincidentally, although McCall seems not to have noticed, Southampton was the home county of Nat Turner, who in 1831 led the most famous slave rebellion in American history.

Nat Turner is a compelling if still mysterious historical memory in Southampton and elsewhere. A God-obsessed Christian preacher, Turner assumed the role of divine agent of retribution against white tyranny. About sixty whites—men, women, children, some in their beds and cradles—died at the hands of Turner and his soldiers. Many significant details of his life and rebellion will ever remain elusive; yet there is some evidence that Turner discriminated among whites, especially by class. Poor whites, he told one lieutenant, were blameless brothers and sisters and should be spared the carnage black rebels wrought upon the countryside that bloody August.[3]

During his involuntary Southampton sojourn, Nathan McCall read Richard Wright, Malcolm X, and other twentieth-century writers. There is scant mention of Turner or other figures in black history in McCall's chilling memoir of 1994, *Makes Me Wanna Holler: A Young Black Man in America.* Nor is there much discrimination by class, whether among whites or blacks. McCall is stunningly unreflective on such matters, and much else. His redemption from criminality—the memoir is a bizarre success story, a version of the Horatio Alger trope—arises from will and pride, a superhuman turning of the same temperament that had led him into captivity.

Race and rage are McCall's subjects. His title—*Makes Me Wanna Holler*—is borrowed from "Inner City Blues," a Marvin Gaye song from the 1970s; but older white readers might also interpret the phrase as an ironic assault upon a rhyme they heard as children: "Eeny, meeny, miney, moe / Catch a nigger

by his toe / If he hollers, let him go / Eeny, meeny, miney, moe."
Such mindless contempt—the unrelenting white insanity—is
McCall's subject. As a junior high school integrationist, young
Nathan suffered trips, taunts, threats. His grades plummeted
as he suffered; so his mother moved him back to a local,
still all-black school. But there was no real escape. In public
places and at work, adult whites humiliated his grandmother
and parents. Television advertising and programming taught
blacks—Nathan included, he writes—to hate themselves. So
the civil rights movement changed little, from the perspective
of someone born in 1955, except to offer opportunity to the
few who could successfully ape white ways, collaborating in a
system more insidious than formal segregation.[4]

McCall's habilitation—not "rehabilitation," he says—was
no compromise, no capitulation. Briefly (but significantly),
he joined the Muslims, borrowing their discipline and Pan-
Africanist confidence. He enrolled in the journalism program
at nearly all-black Norfolk State University. McCall hoped
to avoid the white world—and thus avoid demeaning daily
negotiation and deceit—by working for a black publication,
or perhaps starting his own business. But he could not; his
felony prison record was a problem. Instead, McCall fell into
mondo bianca, working first for the local newspaper, the *Vir-
ginian Pilot-Ledger Star,* then the *Atlanta Journal-Constitution,*
and finally the *Washington Post.* Briefly in Atlanta he tried to
"blend," going so far as to buy and wear a pair of penny-
loafers—the goofiest of "goofy" white apparel. Mostly, McCall
walked a tightrope with a chip on his shoulder, applying himself to his profession and avoiding most contact with whites.[5]
He is a difficult man, touchy and principled.

So what does his remarkable narrative signify? McCall himself, ferociously opinionated but historically unreflective, in-
fers rather than interprets.[6] Like other black male autobiog-
raphers since about 1960, he presents a saga consumed with
pathos—in-prison and out—and a bitter sort of didacticism:
the United States is hell for people of color; white people
are brutal, cruel, manipulative, two-faced, ignorant, arrogant.

Negotiators/Nonnegotiators

11

Sanity necessitates distance from them. Salvation, meanwhile, requires the hardest choices for boys and men—discovery and application of a personal discipline that does not capitulate to whites, and, more important, repudiation of the bloody, premodern black male code of honor.

To Henry Louis Gates Jr., premier academic critic of African-American literature, McCall's book is, most obviously, more doleful evidence that race relations were not much improved by the civil rights movement. "But it's also, more hearteningly," Gates wrote, "about choices—hard ones, yes, but real ones, all the same."[7] *Choices* is that plague-word of the end of the twentieth century, implying (mostly to the affluent, I suspect), mastery over environment and fate, the penultimate bourgeois myth: one *decides* to buy the best product for the money, to adopt a healthful "lifestyle," to overcome adversity, to succeed. (Failure necessitates self-blame.) McCall would probably find these implications harder to swallow, perhaps, than Gates. But willfulness and discipline are not exclusively bourgeois virtues, either. McCall teaches us that even within the painfully narrowed spectrum of options available to the wretched of the earth, moral human choice can make an enormous difference.

Most readers of *Makes Me Wanna Holler* were struck more by salient details of Nathan McCall's story that deviated from the understood norm. Angry ex-convicts usually illustrate the much-examined dislocation and disintegration of the black family since World War II. Without stable adult models and proper guidance, goes the generalization, children go wrong: they join gangs, take to drink and dope, impregnate and get pregnant, commit crimes, and fill the prisons. McCall's parents divorced when he was a small child. His mother's second husband, the sailor who retired to Portsmouth in 1964, was a principled, dutiful worker, a good man and father. It was he who bought the new brick ranch in Cavalier Manor, kept a neat yard and clean car, and tried heroically to instill in his stepsons and sons his ethos of work and constancy. McCall's mother and grandmother were paragons of maternal affection, churchgoing and moral. Other Manor parents, including teachers who also lived there, tried to help with the discipline and safety of all the neighborhood's offspring.

It was an environment not unlike my own white working-class neighborhood, about fifteen years earlier and hardly a mile and a half away, in the very same Portsmouth. McCall's stepfather, upon retirement from the navy, went to work in the shipyard and also, to sustain his growing family, took on part-time work as a freelance gardener. My father worked in the shipyard, then at the Coast Guard base; and he also worked weekends in a gas station pit, greasing cars. McCall and I both were shamed, as boys, to see our elders dirty and subservient, smiling "sir" to patrons standing over them. Both fathers explained that their families needed the money and, equally important, that they took pride in doing well the humblest work. I left Portsmouth and made my way, plagued with class resentments that never quite disappear, to a place in the upper middle class, into brain work at a computer keyboard. Most of my old neighborhood friends remained in the working class; but only one I know of went to prison, and only one was killed—and he in uniform, in Vietnam. McCall's route to brain work and computer keyboards is not only different but also, I will suggest, historically significant. Most of his old "brothers," McCall concludes, "are either in prison, dead, drug zombies, or nickel-and-dime hustlers. Some are racing full-throttle toward self-destruction."[8] Even on his family's quiet street, of the ten households with young males in McCall's time there, four had sons go off to prison.

Pathos had come to black suburbia, and McCall could not explain the phenomenon, either in his memoir or in dozens of postpublication interviews,[9] except to conclude that white racism was responsible for black men's construction of a protective code of machismo, of "coolness," which exaggerated personal dignity and autonomy and encouraged lives of violence outside "the system." This conclusion seems to me both true and utterly unsatisfactory. Stag O'Lee belongs to rural Georgia at the turn of the century, to the Mississippi Delta in John Hurt's youth, and to Chicago's notorious Robert Taylor Homes in the 1960s—not to Cavalier Manor in the 1970s. Stag, incidentally, *was* a "cavalier" in a real sense, as an imperious male operating beyond accepted limits; but he should not be the stepson of a solid Portsmouth shipyard worker. McCall does offer a clue, however. He writes that he consciously repudiated his parents' example in favor of Stag—or more specifically (for McCall never mentions the legendary bad man), in favor of the antihero in *Superfly,* a movie released in 1972. Cruising mean streets to a captivating Curtis Mayfield tune, the flamboyant character "Priest" was an independent businessman, a drug lord actually, who dissed the white world and got away with it. Not a merciless Stag O'Lee, exactly—Priest has a bit of Robin Hood in him—the movie model was there to be assumed, like a seventies "lifestyle" choice, by boys from good homes.[10]

McCall's choice happens to coincide with theologian Cornel West's doleful chronology of "Nihilism in Black America." By "nihilism" West does not mean "a philosophic doctrine that there are no rational grounds for legitimate standards or authority," but rather "the lived experience of coping with a life of horrifying meaninglessness, hopelessness, and (most important) lovelessness." Nihilism results in "a numbing detachment from others and a self-destructive disposition toward the world . . . that destroys both the individual and others." Nihilism of this sort is hardly unprecedented among African Americans, West is well aware. But he senses something changed, something new, since approximately the early 1970s. West's sole social measurement is a dramatic turnabout in the suicide rate of young blacks over the past two decades, from the lowest in the nation to the most rapidly increasing. West's broader, more speculative (but very earnest) analysis focuses on consumerism—or corporate marketers' irresponsible promotion of the "intensification of *pleasure.* . . . comfort, convenience, and sexual stimulation." Cumulatively, the popular culture of consumerism undermines "traditional morality" and its supportive institutions while "edg[ing] out nonmarket values," leaving younger blacks especially "limited capacity to ward off self-contempt" and nihilism.[11]

Nathan McCall and contemporary working-class boys were hardly loveless—disarming part of Cornel West's hypothesis—but in every other respect they seem victims of that merciless, exploitative market, as much as of a hostile white environment. Thus, McCall made his consumerist "choice," and it seems a momentous one, perhaps a historical periodizer. Bad men (and women) there had always been. *Most* African Americans, however, have always valued honest labor and coped with whites where they were obliged. Experience made them master negotiators with the absurdist Caucasian world. McCall and his generation seem, although it is probably too early to say, to have decided *enough:* no more negotiation with the hostile, the implacable, and the insane. They redefine discourse: segregation, integration, assimilation, civil rights, color blindness are all irrelevant. No more collaboration with the crazy. The value of *Makes Me Wanna Holler,* then, may be its demarcation of the end of a centuries-long, perverse dialogue, both between the races and among black people in America. If this is so, now may be a propitious moment to begin appreciation and reassessment of black negotiation, that which is passing or perhaps has already passed.

*A*mong American slaves, performing virtually every conceivable social task for more than two centuries and over an enormous landscape, there were many behavioral modes. Late in the antebellum era, about half of all slaves lived on plantations. A few worked in propinquity with whites; some of those were closely bonded, however problematically, with their masters and mistresses. Most were field hands, working apart from most whites but ever mindful of "the man's" powerful presence. Outside the plantation South, slaves worked alongside white farmer-owners, many of whom, it seems, were tireless and bullying bosses, leaving little space for autonomy. Some slaves worked away from masters in urban factories or in turpentine forests and lumber camps. They were "quasi-free," "quasi" being still a significant modifier. A few slaves escaped captivity for good to the North or to Canada, or to remote places within the South, as maroons. A very few, like Nat Turner, were short-lived messianic rebels. All, save the rebels, lived with some version of tyranny; and generation after generation, they learned and passed on learning of the ways of tyrants. It was education in and of pathos.

If Professor Eugene Genovese is correct—and I am convinced that he is—then the antebellum South was a premodern society, paradoxically locked into production with enslaved labor for a capitalist world market system. Some middle- and upper-class whites were bourgeois, at least "pre-bourgeois," but the prevalent—the hegemonic—culture was antibourgeois. Its justifying and ruling principle in the keeping and governance of slaves was paternalism. Paternalism is much older than racism; but in that the largest productive class was of African descent, racism served the hegemonic class, as it would after slavery's demise. Or as Genovese puts it, the history of the Old South "was essentially determined by particular relationships of class power in racial form." [12]

Both races accepted the ethos of paternalism, but with substantively divergent interpretations. Slaves were to work hard and obey their masters; in return, masters would provide shelter, food, medical care, that is, security. The law of slavery granted owners near-absolute power over property designated as chattel. Yet bondsmen and women were humans with immortal souls, moral selves capable of grace and error, and liable for crimes and misdemeanors. Obedience and security were infinitely pliable notions, almost infinitely problematic, because paternalism is at once a pretext for cruel exploitation and a moral scheme. Most important, and most insidiously, paternalism bound blacks to whites, apprenticed them not only as laborers but also as moral creatures. The latter might achieve salvation in the next world, but the former never freedom, never honor on earth. [13]

The "world" black folks made, then, was defined by tense

contradiction. Slaves demonstrated loyalty while attempting to create personal, family, and spiritual autonomy. Bargaining constantly to expand the definition of masters' obligations, they became masters, themselves, of the arts of concealment and deception. No wonder that more than a century and a quarter after the end of slavery in North America, African Americans number among the world's premier practitioners of verbal play, particularly the double entendre. At once guarded and aggressive, black talk represents an ever-evolving accommodation to a class struggle that is also racial. Slaves "put on ole massa," persuading him who knew them least that he knew them intimately. They negotiated space, in daily and broadly cultural terms, in this manner. The conversation was ever unstable, and ultimately untenable, as the relation between parasites (the slaveholders) and hosts (slaves) must always be.[14]

Perverse negotiations broadened significantly during the Civil War, when southern blacks encountered large numbers of whites (especially men) from the Northeast and Middle West. Good-hearted young missionaries from New England (many of them women) arrived in the South Carolina Sea Islands and other places that fell early into federal hands, determined to deliver to recent plantation slaves basic education and bourgeois notions of free labor and egalitarian citizenship. Yankee soldiers were less often good-hearted, however. Many if not most of them were as contemptuous of black folks as were white southerners; and throughout the broad region, at their work of destruction, Yankees became coercers of labor, felonious assaulters, rapists—more crazy white folks to avoid or, when necessary, to approach with guileful care.[15]

Political Reconstruction after the war elaborated the hard lesson of wariness of Yankees, then, more sadly, added another. Black men became voters, Union-Republican almost to a man and arguably the most loyal of all American voters to the party of Lincoln. White Republican leaders, whether natives or so-called carpetbaggers, assumed this advantage and usually offered the masses of black voters little. Some Republican state governments literally fought the Ku Klux Klan and other conservative white paramilitary organizations. In such instances government, struggling to preserve itself, provided temporary basic protection to black citizens, too. But finally even the federal government—the Grant administration and the Supreme Court—abandoned southern blacks to the mercies of white conservatives. In the meantime the new lesson was that in those few places where Republican rule was long-lived and where a black class system was already intact—Louisiana and South Carolina most obviously—the black bourgeoisie sided with white large property-owners and corporate interests on critical legislative issues that might have benefited the black rural masses.[16]

While the public drama of Reconstruction played to its frustrating final curtain, more long-lasting scenes of negotiation and betrayal took place at the grass roots. Within a year or so after the war, freedmen and -women were obliged to accept the failure of their wartime dream of "Forty Acres and a Mule." The revolution the federal government imposed upon the white South stopped with uncompensated emancipation and conferral of full citizenship upon adult male freedmen. Some blacks acquired property, somehow. Nearly all, however, were without money. So were many white landowners, who now also found themselves without labor. The great economic challenge of the early postbellum era, then, was to reconnect land and labor so that food and commodity production might be resumed—all this in a region largely without banks or cash.[17]

Sharecropping was the great solution. Farms and plantations, previously operated as single production units, were decentralized into ten-to-thirty-acre "farms" to be operated by "renters"—actually laborers, as laws and courts ultimately made clear. Farmers and planters became landlords, collecting as rent half or a third of crops produced, depending upon whether they supplied croppers with animal power and equipment. The system was introduced gradually, piecemeal, throughout the late-1860s and 1870s. And land and labor having been reintroduced, bankers north and south took heart and extended credit to landlords; this would "furnish" them and their renters during the working season. Many large landlords also became in effect both bankers and storekeepers, then, running stores (or "commissaries") on their properties, supplying croppers with basics and a few frills at exorbitant interest rates. Sharecropping, credit, and the expanding railway system explain the threefold expansion of the cotton kingdom during the three decades after 1865.[18]

*S*ince World War II, black Americans have virtually deserted rural America. Black farmers are so rare that their utter extinction is regularly predicted. Part of the explanation for the dramatic urbanization of the black population is a profoundly hateful memory of the humiliations and exploitation associated with sharecropping. So today, in California, Minnesota, Ohio, and New York, among youths two or three generations removed from farming in the Southeast, sharecropping remains a powerful word and image. Ironically, a century and a quarter ago, in the black belts and deltas of the South, it was masterful *black* negotiators who invented the system, for perfectly rational reasons and with high hopes.

On antebellum plantations, slaves worked in gangs and lived in clustered quarters, sometimes virtual barracks. During the war they hoped for their own forty-acre farms, with detached houses—the old yeoman dream of independence and family life. That dashed, freedmen still resisted gang work on centralized plantations, even when planters had cash to pay wages. The standoff ended when planters finally accepted a compromise bargained principally by black would-be farmers: plantations would be subdivided for purposes of production. Old slave houses (or new cabins) would be scattered about on separate plots. Black families would live independently. Many men apparently hoped to keep their women indoors—like white women—except perhaps at harvest, when many hands were needed. Sharecropping was a great improvement over slavery, a fine alternative to free labor in gangs.[19]

But in the long run, sharecropping became more cruel trap than vehicle to autonomy. The world market conspired against the croppers: southerners produced too much of the staple; the British established cotton culture in India and sped supplies to European mills through the new Suez Canal; southerners expanded their own culture further, to compensate. Prices slid, mostly, throughout the late nineteenth century. This prevented operation of the "agricultural ladder" long associated with the North—sharecroppers could not earn profits and ascend to ownership. Indebtedness accumulated, leading some into actual peonage, a version of slavery. But more often, the system and almost perpetual hard times led to the reimposition of paternalism. Forever landlords and creditors, postbellum planters became bosses and patrons to a permanent class of laborers further marked by color. Black men's loss of the right to vote compounded dependency.[20]

Sharecropping and neopaternalism were not slavery: croppers negotiated for farms and terms, and moved often, at their own initiative—by the 1930s, on average, about every other year. But the resemblance was depressing. Croppers seldom saw cash, lived from hand to mouth, and had little or no control over store accounts or the measurement and marketing of crops they made. On many lower Mississippi Valley plantations, landowners even recentralized farm operations, via the so-called through and through system. White foremen on horseback organized black laborers into gangs for plowing, planting, and harvesting. Only thinning and weeding remained for cropper families on their plots. On such plantations (and many others), planters insinuated themselves into croppers' private lives, imposing marital peace or interceding with sheriffs when blacks were accused of misdemeanors. Blacks were reduced to slavelike bargaining for more autonomy within the bounds of paternalism or—unslavelike—taking as much credit as they could get away with, before absconding.[21] Deception in dealing with "the man" was as crucial to survival in 1930 as it had been in 1830.

As late as 1930, a few white planters not only still adhered to the ethos of paternalism but also honestly lived with its obligations.[22] Most, however, seem to have practiced a greedy, mean-spirited, twentieth-century version of nineteenth-century oppression, while claiming to carry burdens of charity and obligation. Their literacy and their control of credit and marketing made systematic cheating of croppers the rule rather than the exception. And in league with bankers and sheriffs, planters sometimes designed and executed the expropriation of black property-owners and their reduction in status from landowner to tenant to sharecropper. Anecdotal evidence of this great fact of the New South's agrarian system is overwhelming, from Virginia's tidewater flats to Georgia's hills to the black belts and deltas of the lower Mississippi Valley.[23]

The most detailed, sustained, and credible black perspective derives from Tallapoosa County, Alabama, in the massive oral history of Ned Cobb. (Theodore Rosengarten, his prompter and amanuensis, discreetly called Cobb, who was illiterate, "Nate Shaw."[24]) The son of a slave, Cobb was a plowhand before adolescence, then a cropper, a tenant (he owned mules and equipment by then), and at last (during the 1920s and early 1930s) a small landowner. Application to business, mastery of mules, and the good luck of having a smart, literate wife explain Cobb's unusual ascent during, as ever, difficult times. Cobb's careful attention to the pitfalls of negotiations with crafty, avaricious whites also contributed to his success. In 1918, for instance, Cobb nearly lost his mules, equipment, and household property when he affixed his mark to a note with a town merchant—without understanding that he was encumbering his own chattels with his landlord's debts. Late that winter Cobb paid his own debt and asked the merchant for his canceled note. The merchant rebuffed him; the landlord cosigner had not yet paid his own obligation. "That was killin' to me," Cobb recollected, because "if he didn't pay . . . they'd come to me for it." Only the landlord could draw upon the account with the merchant, yet Cobb and other tenant cosigners "were all responsible for what he owed."[25] Much later, during the 1940s, a white landlord inquired of Cobb if he knew of a suitable family looking for land to rent. Cobb recommended a white family, but the landlord responded (as Cobb quoted him), "Aw, hell . . . I don't want no damn white man on my place." Cobb reflected upon more than half a century of tenure negotiations: "That teached me fair that a white man always wants a nigger in preference. . . . How come that? How come it for God's sake? He don't want no damn white man on his place. He gets a nigger, that's his glory. He can do that nigger just like he wants to and that nigger better not say nothin against his rulins." Whites, on the other hand, simply "won't take that . . . off another white man."[26]

Briefly, but with larger significance, I think, Cobb had dramatically changed his own mode of negotiation, about fifteen years earlier. When shadowy white Communists founded the Alabama Sharecroppers Union (ASU) during the early 1930s, Cobb, by then a farm owner, joined. He and the ASU aimed to organize croppers and tenants and bargain collectively on their behalf. They would, in other words, impose logical modern labor theory upon a labor system disguised as premodern and paternalist. ASU membership seems to have soared to about 5,500 within a year of the white reds' arrival, although the rank and file were almost certainly all black and non-Communist. The union's one moment of national notoriety arrived when several members, Ned Cobb among them, attempted to prevent Tallapoosa sheriff's deputies from confiscating a tenant's property. There was a shoot-out—Cobb fired several shots—a deputy was wounded, and Cobb went off to prison for a dozen years. The ASU folded in 1935, repressed by the unmovable combined power of landlords, creditors, and lawmen. But its brief existence demonstrated, in the heart of Dixie, a peasantry's eagerness to negotiate as modern people, shucking deceit with the decrepit specter of paternalism.[27]

Industrial-style unionism fared better in the new cotton

plantation country of eastern Arkansas. There, at Tyronza (northwest of Memphis), a dozen men—homegrown white Socialists, black preachers, and farm tenants and croppers —founded the Southern Tenant Farmers' Union (STFU) in July 1934. Like the ASU, they aimed to organize and bargain for landless workers. But by this time, the New Deal had presented an additional dimension to agrarian workers' woes: in order to receive government subsidies, landlords were obliged to reduce cultivated acreage by one-fourth; so they began to evict tenants and croppers. The STFU attempted to halt evictions and have subsidies paid to producers as well as owners; on at least two occasions they led strikes of cotton pickers for higher wages. (The 1936 strike seems to have actually produced better pay.) In the meantime, the union spread northward up the Missouri "Bootheel," eastward and southward into western Tennessee and the Mississippi Delta, and especially westward into Oklahoma, where the STFU attracted not only whites and blacks but also Indians of several nations and Mexican immigrants. Total membership may have reached twenty-five thousand by about 1938. Sadly, within two years the STFU had fractured, and while remnants stayed on, for all practical purposes, the union collapsed—a victim of planters and their allies (as in Alabama), of the government-subsidized resort to mechanized farming, and of internal tensions. Agrarian unionism survived, however, in California and other places, where STFU veterans migrated and resumed the labors of interracial collaboration and unionism.[28]

*W*orld War II hastened the raggedly staged demise of sharecropping, but some remained into the 1960s, even as Nathan McCall's family moved into their new house in Portsmouth's ill-named Cavalier Manor. The South was the last American region to depopulate its rural countryside and substitute machines for mules, men, and women. The recentness of the phenomenon bears repetition and emphasis; for many black southerners, especially, moved directly from sharecropping to sociopathic housing projects in Los Angeles, Chicago, New York, Atlanta, Portsmouth, and countless other burgeoning postwar cities across the nation.[29] Those who remained trapped in the projects in effect skipped the rationality attributed to the modern world at its best, moving from the perversity of the neopaternalist rural South to the nightmarish isolation of Robert Taylor Homes and its many counterparts. Other immigrants to the urban/industrial sectors, however— usually better educated and less encumbered—brought with them a particular lucidity of understanding economic structures and class relationships, and consummate negotiating skills, paradoxically acquired.

Some early black immigrants to industrial America became fodder in the brutal, ethnically complex labor struggles of the late nineteenth and early twentieth centuries. Innocent and hungry, they were scabs, hated by native and immigrant European union workers. But more often, blacks understood instinctively the instrumentality of collective action by men and women workers and became labor radicals. They were members of the Knights of Labor during the 1880s and the Industrial Workers of the World (IWW) before World War I. Recruited to work in the coal mines of northern Alabama and southern West Virginia, they eagerly joined the United Mine Workers. During the great strike of 1920, three-quarters of the miners who struck Alabama pits were black. And during West Virginia's mine wars of the early 1920s, blacks were union mainstays, along with European immigrants.[30]

By this time A. Philip Randolph and Chandler Owen had become intellectual leaders of the American Left. Their remarkable monthly, The Messenger ("The Only Radical Negro Magazine in America"), promoted the "one big union" ideals of the IWW still, in 1919, when government repression had virtually exterminated the syndicalist organization. The "history of the labor movement in America proves," they wrote, "that the employing class recognize no race lines. They will exploit a white man as readily as a black man. They will exploit women as readily as men. They will even go to the extent of coin-

ing the labor, blood, and suffering of children into dollars."
In 1925 Randolph, who was southern-born, organized the all-black Brotherhood of Sleeping Car Porters, but throughout the interwar period and beyond, he ceaselessly promoted an end to racial discrimination in the union movement.[31]

Beginning in 1933, the CIO—the Committee (then Congress) of Industrial Organizations—provided semiskilled workers white and black their great opportunity. Thrown together in the great rubber, steel, and auto-manufacturing centers, European ethnics grappled with native migrants from the South for precious jobs. CIO leaders, many of them Socialists or Communists, preached solidarity. Ensuing struggles both for worker solidarity and union recognition often demonstrated blacks' historical advantage. White Appalachian-born workers were usually shocked by the color-blind ferocity of employers' resistance. "People fight against us Southern whites," declared a female Detroit auto worker. "We are on the same basis as Negroes." Blacks, on the other hand, immediately perceived northern industrial oppression as the counterpart of the rural South. Bad bosses were "slave drivers" or "Ku Klux Klan" members. Generally, too, black workers were quicker to accept collectivity as ideal and instrument. This seems especially true in Detroit and Flint during the late 1930s struggles to win recognition for the United Auto Workers (UAW). Arguably the most progressive of the larger CIO unions, especially on racial subjects, the UAW represented to blacks not only worker solidarity but also their best connection to the Democratic Party (their new political home) and to a burgeoning civil rights movement.[32]

During and especially after World War II, the labor movement expelled left radicals and distanced itself somewhat from civil rights. (Randolph's Sleeping Car Porters and Walter Reuther's UAW were exceptions.) The cold war was underway at home and abroad. Nonetheless, throughout these years of more conservative "big unionism," black workers were consistently more faithful to labor organizations than their white counterparts. Class-based activism—as opposed to race-based

—was weakened already, then, before industrial America was transformed into a "Rust Belt" during the 1970s and 1980s. Proud old industrial unions were undercut, then brought to their knees during the eighties by the Reagan administration's antilabor program. By this time American politicians and most labor leaders seemed incapable of class analysis. Instead, whether Democrat or Republican, they were preoccupied with a presumably vast black "underclass," saturated with illegal drugs and guns, feeding upon itself.[33] This was Nathan McCall's world, the context for his values, perceptions, "choices."

*W*hile still at the Southampton Correctional Institution, McCall writes, he finally "discovered that . . . [manual] work wasn't so bad after you got used to it. I realized that it's your attitude about the work you do that can determine how pleasant or unpleasant it is. For the first time, I understood what my stepfather meant when he said there was dignity in all work." But one is not quite convinced. McCall seems more to have accommodated himself to coercion, prudently minimizing the rage he had felt before. Nonetheless, he writes that he wished to communicate his discovery to his stepfather, during a prison visit; "words formed in my mind," he confessed, but "wouldn't come out." Writing of a few years before, when his stepfather had made him and his brothers work at their house and help him garden in Sterling Point, an affluent white suburb of Portsmouth, McCall recalled the formation of a different ethic that, despite the prison epiphany, more or less still informs his life.[34]

This was the generational contrast. His "stepfather's life was controlled by work," McCall reflected. "It was all he'd ever known. He'd grown up on a farm in Milledgeville, Georgia, where he did backbreaking labor every day and learned to master with his hands skills that most college-educated people never learned." McCall "marveled at the things he could do"— auto and household repairs, construction and masonry—even as Nathan and his brothers "hated him sometimes for trying to work us to death." McCall's lasting confusion derived from conjoining his stepfather's preachment, "If you work hard, you can get anything you want in life," with the vision of the man and boys weeding Sterling Point's azalea gardens. "Coming from the Deep South," McCall decided, "my stepfather believed that you had to ignore all the shit that white people dished out and learn to swallow pride for survival's sake. Cut from the civil rights mold, *he believed blacks could overcome racism by slaving hard and making do with what little they had.*"[35] McCall seems ignorantly to conflate Booker T. Washington's ethics of work and patience with an inconsistent "civil rights mold." And one wonders if the stepfather ever actually declared that diligence would "overcome racism," anyway. I rather doubt it. So McCall's misunderstanding of his stepfather's message seems to have foreclosed the possibility of McCall's learning some of his elders' most important experiences—with working-class pride, workplace comradeship, and the *intrinsic* satisfaction of labor well executed. Instead, color overwhelms class in McCall's thinking, and with it, the possibility of refocusing the black tradition of constructive negotiation. One can hardly dismiss McCall; but his is a sad development, indeed.

Forces larger than McCall's experience militate against clear perception of class in this country. The white myth of equal opportunity associated with small-"r" republicanism survives its remote origins. In the broad Middle West, in particular, republicanism by the middle of the last century blossomed into a thriving bourgeois culture—long since nationalized—where recognition and mention of social class is considered poor manners at best, or more often, subversive.[36] The Democratic Party continues to harbor most of what remains of the American labor movement, but its commitment to bourgeois culture seems only marginally less extreme than the Republicans'. Then there is the African-American intelligentsia. Usually people of some privilege, themselves, yet denied access to conventional power, they have often expressed strategies of racial solidarity rather than class consciousness and advocacy. To them hardly less than to Nathan McCall, the pervasiveness and persistence of white racism confer logic and justification upon class-blind color-consciousness.[37]

So in *Makes Me Wanna Holler,* when McCall encounters class he is usually caustic but unable to see beyond brutal racial stereotypes and his own social discomfort. In Atlanta and in Washington, D.C., he encountered in newsrooms upper-middle-class blacks. McCall thought "these Atlanta blacks were different from most blacks I'd spent any real time around. Many had come from staunchly middle-class backgrounds and were second-generation college graduates. Some were stone-cold assimilationists, who had done everything the white man said you needed to do to blend in and get ahead." Those with degrees from the most prestigious white universities were the most "pitiful"—"the ones who surrendered so completely to white domination that they were alien to themselves. Racism was so painful for them that they denied its existence." Washington had a "more entrenched black middle class[,] . . . more assertive and politically astute." Yet "On the other hand, they are illustrations of a widely held view of middle-class blacks everywhere: In spite of all their money, skills, and potential, they're one of the most confused, alienated groups in the land. Middle-class blacks in D.C. are some of the most bourgeois, pretentious, snooty black folks I've seen anywhere."[38]

McCall preferred the "funky barbershop" crowd "in a serious working-class neighborhood" in Washington. Working-class to McCall, however, seems to bear no relationship to *work.* In his favorite barber shop, for instance, he suspected that "half the barbers" and a good number of the clientele were ex-cons. McCall liked their slang, their "crazy" talk. "Crazy" as in Cavalier Manor's "crazy niggers," who are not so much working-class—men like his stepfather—as they are, like McCall in an earlier life, neo–Stag O'Lees.[39] Having come so far, he has never quite left Cavalier Manor, that place where too many men born during the 1950s repudiated their elders and the challenges of negotiating the slippery business of race and class.

*S*till, Cavalier Manor is not the world entire; and significant as Nathan McCall may be, he does not represent everyone in his cohort. Other black men and women—primarily creatures of the upper middle class McCall mocks—persist in negotiation.[40] They do so in ways appropriate to a "post–civil rights" era, understanding rage but eager, even desperate, to achieve both structural changes and cultural accommodations that will heal. Among the contemporary intelligentsia, Cornel West (born in 1953, in Tulsa) combines historical knowledge, Marxian analysis, and liberal Protestant theology to elaborate a "prophetic" synthesis of that which is African, American, Christian, and progressive. West neither despises nor separates himself from white people.[41] West's Harvard colleague, Henry Louis Gates, Jr. (born in 1950), the brilliant explicator of African and African-American language, is literally married into the white world and is the father of mixed-racial daughters. This situation alone obliges negotiations too complex and profound for most of us to imagine. The richness—perhaps the oddness, too—of Gates's life may help explain why, in a little memoir portentously entitled *Colored People,* published just months after Nathan McCall's book, Gates extends black experimentation with the language of identity with a view to reconcile black folks not only with themselves but also with all us whites who may be willing to read, to listen.

Superficial similarities between Gates's and McCall's early circumstances of life are striking. Gates's family was strong, intact, and working-class, in Piedmont, West Virginia, a paper mill town in the Potomac Valley near Cumberland, Maryland. His father, son of Maryland farmers and Cumberland professional men, got little education; and at the Piedmont mill, like other blacks, he was allowed only unskilled work on the loading platform. Evenings he spent at his second job as janitor at the local telephone company. Gates's mother was a command-ing, loving presence. She was a churchwoman, renowned for her eulogies at funerals, her dignified carriage, her intelligence, her ambition for her sons. Gates and his older brother did not work with their father, but they were disciplined to family responsibilities at home. They also watched a great deal of television and listened to popular music. But unlike McCall and his friends, neither Gates boy succumbed to the consumer market poison that Cornel West identifies as a major source of black nihilism, rage, and self-destruction.[42] The Gateses' seeming imperviousness to nihilism is but the beginning of their differences from McCall and his Portsmouth comrades.

It may be that Henry Louis Gates's five years' seniority to McCall—as well as the enormous differences between Piedmont and Portsmouth—is a significant reason for the former's success in accommodating himself to *mondo bianca*. Gates's first years were spent securely in the age of segregation, in the caress of a small, fascinating, and witty community of mutually supportive, clannish black folks. Piedmont had a white social hierarchy, but blacks were virtually all working-class renters—they were not "allowed" to own property until the 1970s.[43] Gates began elementary school the year after Piedmont's schools were desegregated. Like Nathan McCall, he was studious and smart; but in personable little Piedmont, Gates and his brother were members of a relatively unthreatening minority, and his parents were well known and respected by whites. (Portsmouth's blacks approximately equalled whites in number, and the city's scale permitted the quality of personability only within race- and class-specific neighborhoods.) Mrs. Gates became the first black PTA officer in the unified school system. Gates's older brother, meanwhile, a stellar athlete as well as student, suffered more of integration's stress, paving the way for young Louis (or "Skip," or "Skippy," as he was called). Indeed, Skip seems to have been rather a pet to white teachers and many classmates. He also reciprocated puppy love with his elementary school's other academic whiz, a white girl, until, approaching adolescence, they were separated by community pressures. Civil rights agitation, meanwhile, hardly touched northern West Virginia. White school boards had yielded to desegregation early; then practically nothing happened until the late-1960s—Gates's teen years—when craft unions inside the mill admitted black workers from the loading platform. The stylish ideology of black power, however, compelled the young. Skip Gates foreswore taming his hair, cultivating an "Afro," and he argued endlessly with his father over racial politics, his preference for "black" over "Negro" or (worse) "colored." As a first-year student at Potomac State College, a nearby school affiliated with West Virginia University, Gates deliberately challenged segregation at a popular bar/dance hall, risking serious injury to himself and his companions. (The bar closed when the white owner refused to admit black patrons.) Gates was just old enough, then, to have become a civil rights militant, at the end of what is conventionally called the movement, before his transfer to Yale University and departure from the border South.

Gates has no more left Piedmont than McCall has deserted Cavalier Manor, however. Both men go home, literally and literarily. Yet the differences in place and experience upon the two are enormous. Gates's Piedmont is mellow, "sepia" in his memory, bittersweet only because the town has declined with the mill's reduced capacity, and because integration diminished or destroyed black institutions and rituals that nourished his youth—the church, the millworkers' annual "colored pic-a-nic." But Gates understands that history is change, all too often tragic, bittersweet at best. Irreparable losses counterpoint gains. He understands, too, with Cornel West and especially Edward Said that cultures conflict, react to one another, bend, blur, define, and redefine themselves. So Gates the African American—with European ancestors in his father's line, African-European descendants in his own—will explain the dynamic with wisdom and tender humor. His is the legitimacy, then, to suggest reconsideration of the old identifying expression, "colored people," now of course without condescension or apology, but with sympathy, affection, and a measure of descriptive accuracy.

One wishes that Gates's powerful sympathy and mastery of language extended to the lower strata of white society as well. This may be too much to ask of him, remembering the snarling mouths and flailing fists of young working-class white men who assaulted him and his friends at the Swordfish bar/dance hall in 1969, or countless other wounds and slights Gates does not elaborate. But elsewhere in his memoir, where perception and description without fear or anger seem appropriate, Gates is simply the snob. He had delighted, at ten, in his discovery that the Cumberland Gateses—his father's Howard- and Harvard-educated relatives—were upper-middle-class. Piedmont's least privileged whites, meanwhile, are just "trash"—the usage lacking the affectionate irony he clearly associates with "nigger" and "coon." And rural folk from the "hollers" are "crackers," "hillbillies," or more commonly, "rednecks."[44]

Gates should understand, one must think, that these people are no more two-dimensional than his own beloved family and neighbors; that they have poignant histories, too, and strengths to balance failings, intrinsic human value and immortal souls. Yet I concede that ordinary whites seem often to confound sympathetic understanding. They are both ubiquitous and utterly mysterious. The next two essays, then, will approach these folks—incompletely and inadequately I fear—but with the attention to dimensional depth and political-economic context they deserve, like any other people.

Retro Frontiersmen

Jackson businessman: "You know, I like those rednecks. They're so laid back.
They don't give a shit. They don't give a shit."
V. S. Naipaul: "Is that because they're descendants of pioneers?"
Businessman: "There's no question about it. They're descendants of
pioneers. They're satisfied to live in those mobile homes. . . . They ain't got
fifteen damn cents, and they're just tickled to death."
V. S. Naipaul in Mississippi,
ca. 1988

*I*n the course of his long, clockwise "turn in the South" during the late-1980s, V. S. Naipaul, the perambulating British writer, discovered a disquieting crisis looming in Mississippi. Curiously, it was not another racial conflict, but a crisis linking landscape and social class. So-called rednecks, Naipaul learned, already pushed from outdated farms into mortgaged trailers on rented plots, were now being squeezed from beloved wilderness recreation areas.

"Redneck" men had "a nice life," Naipaul's informant told him, "but it depends on a natural life being available. I would say that if those rednecks didn't have these natural surroundings in Mississippi—because the outdoor thing's their favorite pastime—they would be very bored. And hunting rights are becoming so valuable now, they're going to be forced out of the market within five years." Affluent men had come up from Louisiana and down from the North to shoot Mississippi's "big deer" and abundant ducks, organizing hunting clubs and posting most of the woodlands. "I bet you couldn't drive forty-five minutes out of Jackson," the informant declared, "without finding land that wasn't leased. It's going to have a 'Posted' sign. . . . One day there's going to be a killing about it, I tell you."[1]

Actually, as Naipaul's colorful informant spoke, violent class conflict was not a rhetorical prospect but already a fact of southern life. For in the second half of the twentieth century, even as the United States entered what is called its postindustrial age, Americans, especially southerners, began to reenact medieval European struggles between the privileged and the excluded over forests. Warfare was (and remains) more often furtive, guerrillalike revenge-making rather than the direct, confrontational sort. Firing posted woodlands is its most common expression. The combatants are neither organized nor articulate in the usual sense; there are few written manifestos. Nor is there much articulate recognition of the warfare from the privileged. Admission of danger and disorder is, of course, bad public relations, anathema to governments, corporations, chambers of commerce. So one must learn to "read" the warfare in other sources—especially the lamentations of professional foresters, who record the persistence of arson with weary frustration. More than forty years after Hank Williams Sr. performed his paean to incindiarism, "Settin' the Woods on Fire," southerners remain the nation's premier forest arsonists.[2]

Firing forests was for many generations a folk behavior instrumental—even essential, one might argue—to the practice of agriculture. The aborigines cleared crop fields by girdling and burning trees; Euro- and Afro-Americans adapted the method to their own modified European and African systems of farming.[3] Setting woods afire was criminalized only early in this century, at a critical stage of ordinary southerners' alienation from access to woodlands. This particular alienation was very protracted in its development. One might properly suggest it as yet another result of the Civil War, but the late antebellum era had presented its own version of a comprehensive attack upon poor men's notions of the commons and the appropriateness of fire on their own and others' woodland properties. All this notwithstanding, my argument shall be that ordinary white southerners' deprivation of wilderness is a very recent discontinuity in southern history; that is, that a large proportion of southern whites remained, well into this century, relatively independent from many things modern— money, technology, government, and perhaps most important, supervision at work. They lived on "frontiers"[4] in unexpected places until hardly more than a generation ago.

*A*t the end of 1852, Frederick Law Olmsted descended from New York into Virginia. Olmsted began this first of his legendary journeys in the slave states with an attitude—that of an "honest growler." The son of a Connecticut merchant, he had already crossed two oceans, studied modern agronomy, and established a commercial farm on Staten Island. Olmsted was bourgeois: he expected efficiency in public transportation and business; he assumed that agriculture was another business, serving markets (he himself sold cabbages to Manhattanites); and he carried a watch, consulting it often. Olmsted was also a fine amateur naturalist who admired the contrived order of European parks and gardens, as well as the symmetry of row-crops on permanent fields. So in the South, beginning with central and southeastern Virginia, Olmsted waxed growlier, more the nineteenth-century counterpart of our discommoded contemporaries who travel in the so-called Third World (or perhaps Italy), where nothing arrives on time, inefficiency reigns, and most of the natives are indifferent to discipline and order.[5]

Historians are accustomed to employing Olmsted's journals and letters to illustrate slavery's illogic. Plantation slavery's dynamics were indeed a principal subject to the traveler, but there is more. For Olmsted was often on horseback, occasionally lost, in backcountry beyond the pale of the great estates that enthralled (sometimes appalled) his Yankee readers. Here his keen observation (among many other sources) helps us reconstruct a culture that ordinary white southerners had created in the seventeenth century and that thrived, still, at the end of the antebellum period.

First, there were trees—virtually all pines—and packs of feral hogs, running, according to Olmsted, as if after foxes. During his first such ride, east of Petersburg, Virginia (probably in lower Prince George County), in December 1852, Olmsted noticed that old deciduous trees remained only next to ravines and other rough places unsuitable for farming. Everywhere else there were almost endless reaches of conifers—probably loblollies—in patches of varying heights, all the trees in each patch about the same size. Olmsted understood that such landscapes indicated a shifting system of agriculture, wherein fields were regularly abandoned and new fields created, with fire, from woodlands that a generation or so before had been cropped a few years, then abandoned to natural succession. So here, in one of the longest settled parts of English-speaking America, the European scheme of permanent crop-fields—familiar to Olmsted not only in Europe but also in his native New England and in New York—was well established only among the most affluent riverside planters.[6]

Fleet razorbacks elaborate the portrait. Long-legged, high-bodied, and of various colorations, hogs swarmed loose everywhere—much as Robert Beverley had complained in his famous *History* of 1705. In Beverley's time, when the coastal plain was still almost formally a frontier, colonial assemblies had sought to reconcile agriculture, free-range animals, and wilderness with laws requiring high fences about cropfields—not cattle and hogs. A century and a half later, Olmsted observed, little had changed; Tidewater Virginia remained frontierish, much to his dismay.[7]

Such eastern frontiers were possible only when others, to the west, beckoned surpluses of human population. Nineteenth-century coastal plains demographic history is stunningly flat. Women succeeded in producing huge broods of offspring, as they had since the late seventeenth century; but after the Revolution, populations in the East remained more or less constant. Manuscript agricultural censuses reveal the benefits to those who remained in the coastal plain, and the foundation of the shifting system of farming Olmsted and others observed. Most all whites were proprietors of farms of some size and on virtually all of these, hardly ever was as much as half the land placed under cultivation or in pasturage. Families, then, depending on their composition and desires, had the option of shifting the sites of their cropfields. To them the woodlands were future reserves that, in the meantime, harbored and nourished cattle and hogs. Demography and landscape in such a configuration provided both security and ease.[8]

Olmsted was unsympathetic, however; farmers seemed careless and lazy to him. With disciplined effort, he believed, they might have produced more, on permanent fields. Olmsted had southern, nonbourgeois company in this judgment, among progressive riverfront planters and editors of farm magazines. Most important among them was Edmund Ruffin, who had done much to found modern American agronomy in the very county where Olmsted first saw old-field pines and speedy Virginia razorbacks.

The young Ruffin had had compelling reasons of his own— not Olmsted's more abstract hunger for efficiency—to become production-oriented on permanent cropfields. Inheriting a James River farm in 1813 that had been worked already by at least two generations, Ruffin married and promptly fathered no fewer than eleven children, nine of whom survived. There were also about fifty slaves to be fed from the farm's worn soils. Ironically, Ruffin read Thomas Malthus (among many other learned authors) while his poor wife and he created a Malthusian nightmare. He thought of abandoning his patrimony for new land in the West, but unable to find a buyer, he bent himself to making his farm adequate to growing, growing demand.[9]

So Ruffin read inappropriate British and immature American agronomy, tried his best, and failed, until he discovered Sir Humphry Davy's new lectures in agricultural chemistry. Through these he came to understand the nature of soil acidity and apply it to his own land. Calcium in the form of fossil shells (marl) or lime would fix nitrogen in such soils and revive fecundity. There were thinly covered banks of marl on Ruffin's own property—an elderly slave revealed the first of these to him—so Ruffin began to restore his lands. He fed his huge white and black families, earned profits on surpluses, and remained in the Old Country, married to his version of European agronomy and to the institution of slavery, which made possible his ingenious but labor-intensive system.[10]

Ruffin's success with soil chemistry led him further into reformism that attacked prevailing folkish practice. Most important, after marling, was Ruffin's assault upon the old fence law. With compelling rationality, he questioned the wisdom of maintaining extensive wooden enclosures about cropfields, when farm animals might be penned with less expense and less impact on dwindling timber supplies. Ruffin was unsympathetic to the criticism that poor people could not feed cattle and hogs denied the range, and he was enraged that Virginia's General Assembly was overwhelmingly persuaded by the criticism. Likewise, Ruffin was impatient with the persistence of old laws permitting empoundments of streams and construction of small mills. His concern was public health: millponds harbored the cause of disease, malaria in particular. The mills themselves, capable of operation only brief periods each year, Ruffin dismissed as mere "amusements" for common men. That such little mills might still have utility to ordinary farmers, grinding their corn into meal during seasonal freshets—and avoiding dependence on owners of large, year-round mills—was of no concern to Ruffin.[11]

Meanwhile, across the South, other men of his class—editors such as New Orleanian J. D. B. DeBow and labor-rich planter-politicians such as South Carolinian James Henry Hammond—hailed Edmund Ruffin and his reforms. He became famous, invited to write, to speak, to geologize afield, and to spread reform to other states. The fame and attendant travel prepared the way for Ruffin's political mischief of the 1850s, which led to Fort Sumter and the holocaust of 1861–65. Yet in the meantime, at least as early as the early 1850s,

Ruffin properly counted himself a failure as reformer. Only a tiny minority of South Atlantic riverside planters adopted marling. The open range remained intact, and the countryside remained dotted with little mills and their stagnant ponds.[12] Then hundreds of thousands of woods-burning, hog-running, mill-tinkering farmers flocked to Confederate ranks, perhaps thinking they were defending their independent way of life as much as anything.

If this were so, then the Civil War acquires additional irony. For it marks the beginning of the protracted destruction of ordinary white southerners' rustic independence. Modern agronomy could not do them in, yet: there was so little education, so little money, for so long after the war. Instead, a vast postbellum expansion of the Cotton Kingdom fueled by commercial fertilizers—especially guano—rather than marl, gradually pushed them into the world of specialization and money. (Marl was "free" to coastal farmers with the labor to dig it.) Railroads organized the countryside and delivered growing tenancy rates as surely as they delivered guano and specialization. Before the end of the nineteenth century, considerable numbers of whites were beginning to occupy dependent statuses previously identified only with black freedmen.[13]

Rather, it was the sudden loss of cattle and hogs, then the loss of the forests, that set vice-jaws grinding slowly together upon them. In 1860, according to the federal census, there were twice as many hogs as humans in the Virginia-Carolina low country where Edmund Ruffin lived and roamed. Elsewhere in the South, where there were no cities, the preponderance of pigs was much higher. Five years after the war, when another census was taken, there were fewer hogs than people in Ruffin's old country. Swine populations improved periodically thereafter, but the South never recovered the 1860 figure, even as the number of humans soared. Several millions of new African-American farmers, meanwhile, began their freedom without sustaining livestock. And white farmers also found themselves buying meat from the surpluses of the Middle West.[14]

Retro Frontiersmen

39

The gradual alienation of forests was even more part of a vast national tragedy. Conflict with Plains Indians was underway before the Civil War was finished. Buffalo herds that sustained aboriginal culture were systematically slaughtered during the following decade. An enormous, but virtually treeless, territory now lay open for farming and city-building. So timber entrepreneurs—Frederick Weyerhaeuser is best remembered among the hordes—began to clear-cut the forests of the Great Lakes states and simultaneously to stake huge claims to federal and private woodlands in the Southeast. Weyerhaeuser owned rights across the continent, ultimately including enormous holdings in eastern North Carolina and the lower Mississippi Valley. His and other new woodsmen's employment of the railroad, then other modern technologies, revolutionized the timber business.[15]

Before the appearance of the new men, timber-getting had been largely winter work for farmers and other rural men with other employment. They favored, of course, mature hardwoods growing by roads, or more often, by rivers and creeks, which they used in getting dressed trees home or to markets. Postbellum entrepreneurs' employment of rails was revolutionary because railroads permitted timber-getting—especially the devastating practice of clear-cutting—beyond the banks of watercourses.

Chowan County, North Carolina, demonstrates the impact. In 1880, according to a local historian, the county's forests were "virgin"—save along the Chowan and Perquimans rivers, which mark the county's lateral boundaries. But that year two rail lines from Virginia approached Chowan and, ahead of the construction crews, their agents penetrated, buying up timber rights at twenty-five cents per one thousand board feet. The railroads followed; and by 1890, Chowan's forests were cut out. Small local sawmillers fed on leftover scraps for another decade; then there was nothing for another generation.[16]

Elsewhere, especially in the Gulf States, the history of the Lake States cutout was repeated between about 1890 and 1910. Lumbermen shipped records of board feet from southern forests during these years that have never been equalled since and probably *could* never be equalled again. The cutout was so devastating that larger operators who intended to continue in the business—such men as John Henry Kirby of East Texas and John L. Roper of Norfolk, Virginia—began to organize the industry with a view to restraining harvests, maintaining prices, and establishing conservationist forestry practices. By this time, too, Gifford Pinchot of Pennsylvania, a graduate of Yale and of a European forestry school, had been called to the Biltmore estate near Asheville, North Carolina. Pinchot initiated fire-prevention and sustained yield management in this vast private forest and began the training of a corps of young American foresters who would soon staff new corporate and state forest management bureaus across the nation, especially in the South. These experts served the designs of such lumbermen as Kirby and Roper, becoming arguably the principal enemies of the traditional folk agronomy.[17]

Professional forestry, imported from Europe, aimed to manage woodlands for sustained yield. Implementation followed the two principal canons that experts pursue, for the most part, even to this day: suppression of fire and reforestation with commercial seedlings (i.e., the practice of monoculture). Remnant populations of field-shifting farmers, then, along with "arsonists" who, like the aborigines employed fire in hunting, became professional foresters' problems. During the progressive era and after, states created forestry bureaus, tree nurseries, and fire patrols. Setting fires became illegal, so foresters became policemen, allied with sheriffs in the suppression of criminalities old and new: arson in several manifestations, and moonshining, which involved fire that sometimes got out of hand.[18]

The appearance of professional foresters corresponded to the creation of the U.S. Department of Agriculture's Cooperative Extension Service and the posting of yet more experts— the "county agents"—in every rural county. Agents, like foresters, were mostly college men who were modern, scientific, and devoted to management and mastery of nature. In them, especially, Edmund Ruffin triumphed posthumously: farming was a business to be conducted for profit at markets. Crop-fields were to be permanent, sustained-yield factories, maintained by applied science. This included, on acidic landscapes, application of lime or marl. Farm animals were to be confined, the better to improve breeds, weights, and profits. Folk agronomy was "ignorance" to be overcome by teaching and legal repression. So the new, "scientific" agronomists' canons converged with forestry: the open range must be closed where it still existed; firing woods was criminal mischief. In North Carolina, county agents formally joined forces with the state's Forestry Association to prevent cotton farmers from setting fires, in the mistaken belief that boll weevils wintered in the woods. Experts combined were irresistible, and Carolina's near-ancient open range was at last closed just after World War I.[19]

$\mathcal{T}$he great vice was not yet closed, nonetheless. By the time North Carolina's range was officially ended, a postwar commodity price collapse threw farmers across the nation into depression. Impoverished farmers might with their own labor continue certain "scientific" practices; but in the main, the new agriculture espoused by the agents required investments of scarce money. Seldom, even in prosperous times, had agents invested their time and effort in small freeholders or tenants, anyway; large operators inclined to adopt labor-saving machinery were the agents' pets. So would they continue. Rural America, meanwhile, stagnated and began to shrink with out-migration—that is, except in the South. There, a rural birth-rate reminiscent of Chinese demography burgeoned. And despite certain cracks, the national labor market remained closed to southerners white and black, through most of the 1930s.[20]

So millions of rural southerners were entrapped through most of two endless decades of agricultural depression. Most worked in unmechanized corn, tobacco, and cotton cultures, producing surpluses but seldom seeing cash. A substantial minority of southerners persisted in, or returned to, a rural world hardly connected to markets at all. Here was a geographically dispersed yet coherent, self-sufficient South, where at least half of everything produced on farms was consumed at home. Most of the farms classified as self-sufficient in 1930 were clustered in the Appalachian highlands—in eastern and southern West Virginia, southwestern Virginia, eastern Kentucky and Tennessee. Another large group was Ozarkian—northwestern Arkansas and adjacent northeastern Oklahoma. But other "primitive" southern counties were scattered in western Kentucky and Tennessee, in upper piedmont and tidewater Virginia, and in the sandy "wiregrass" country of southeastern Georgia, northern Florida, southern Mississippi, and eastern Texas.[21]

Whether upland or lowland, self-sufficient farmers worked the poorest land in the South. Their cash incomes were comparable to those of sharecroppers in the commodity-producing black belts and delta subregions. Often these farmers actually saw *less* cash than croppers; and New Dealers would shortly call them woefully impoverished, as they indeed were by the standards of the urban middle classes. Yet most of these white folks (plus a few blacks) *owned* their poor farms and enjoyed an isolation and independence unknown in the plantation South. Ignored by the Extension Service, many of them—we cannot know how many—were able to persist in traditional ways, ignored, it would seem, by the foresters as well. Speaking of Clay County, West Virginia, during the 1920s, one native recalled, about 1976, that "everybody had the woods full a hogs. Just turned them out and let them nibble on the mas[t]." Each fall, he reported, men with "big dogs" would "go out and catch these hogs" for fattening and slaughter. "We didn't want for anything to eat them days," he said.[22]

Still, isolation was hardly complete, the world not too distant. Self-sufficient farmers fed themselves, fed animals free in the forests, traded labor among neighbors. But they still had cash requirements, however modest: for coffee and sugar, workstock and some tools, taxes, and to support their little

Retro Frontiersmen
43

churches. They raised the money in a variety of ways: Appalachian men often left home during winters for factory work in the Middle West. Or they "raised coal" nearer home from walk-in slope mines. Upland and lowland men performed winter "public work" at sawmills and lumber camps. Some made a little whiskey. Women sold or traded eggs and quilts and other crafts at tiny country stores. No doubt a few acquired a taste for modern consumption and never returned to this quaint South. Most sojourners seem never to have perceived "public work" as more than temporary, however—a strategy to maintain a rural home, to protect independence, to avoid supervision at work other than by a senior family member.[23]

$\mathscr{T}$he white poor and near-poor in the rich-land commodity sections of the region are harder to generalize about. Some found opportunity—the hope, at least, of independence—in the ruin of long-cropped cotton country, such as the Georgia Black Belt. Banks and insurance companies that foreclosed on worn-out plantations invited "hard scrabble" farmers, who were often white migrants from the southern uplands, to rent or buy subdivided plots. Such places became whiter, demographically, during the 1930s, as landless blacks decamped for the North or, more likely, for better renting prospects to the west. The "hard scrabble" settlers, meanwhile, apparently tried to subsist, extending the culture of the self-sufficient South.[24]

But many more whites—their numbers mounting steadily— lost independence and hope, suffering a descent into life and labor under others' supervision. How *much* supervision (or actual tyranny) whites endured is as problematical as the subject of the psychic distress they must have suffered. Many thousands of whites fell socially to the status of sharecropper, more a mere laborer than a "tenant" in the customary sense, and a status originally conceived for ex-slaves—all this in a white-supremacist culture. Because blacks were generally without the vote and the protection of the law, more likely to be illiterate, and accustomed to white superiors' discipline, white landlords almost universally preferred black tenants and sharecroppers. In the black belts and delta areas, with their enormous black majorities, landlords directed the plowing, planting, and harvesting of their plantations virtually as though the land were not subdivided into cropper plots, and they insinuated themselves oppressively into workers' personal and productive lives.[25]

Yet for a while during the 1930s, white sharecroppers actually outnumbered blacks. Whites began to replace black croppers during World War I, as blacks took advantage of their first important opportunity in northern labor markets. There is but a little anecdotal evidence that white pioneer workers in plantation country suffered the same, manipulative supervision blacks had for generations. Later, landlords in the black belts and deltas were the first to invest New Deal subsidies in labor-saving machinery, beginning the transformation of their plantations into western-style food and fiber factories. In the meantime, however, the white majority of sharecroppers seems to represent not so much white incursions into black belts and deltas so much as the immiserization of hill-country farmers. Here, both race relations and farm tenancy were different. Most of the piedmont South was white majority. Landlords may have preferred black tenants and croppers but were constrained to take on white families, most of whom farmed without supervision, kept their own accounts, and marketed their own surpluses. Depending upon local circumstances, too, hill-country whites were able to keep cattle and hogs, raise their own vegetables, and feed themselves—matters essential to any construction of "independence."[26] Probably owing to whites' situational advantages as tenants, then, historians are constrained to find among them much of a recognizable "class" consciousness, or a sense of historical direction, much less expression of brother- and sisterhood with African Americans in similar circumstances.

The great exception was in northeastern Arkansas during the mid- and late-1930s, where the Southern Tenant Farmers'

Union enjoyed a brief but spectacular life. It was an odd place, inviting the exceptional. As recently as World War I, much of northeastern Arkansas was wooded swampland, barely inhabited. Then developers clear-cut the lumber, drained the swamps, and sold the alluvial land, mostly in enormous tracts, to wealthy individuals and corporations. They, in turn, attracted masses of immigrant tenants and sharecroppers (especially the latter), black and white, from the upper and lower South. This was the last cotton frontier in eastern America, then, a country of strangers who came to virgin land with high hopes. These were soon dimmed by abysmal cotton prices, then dashed by the New Deal's Agricultural Adjustment Act, which inadvertently provoked massive evictions of tenants and croppers by landlords who had to reduce production in order to receive government subsidies.[27]

A strange and marvelous cabal of white Socialists and black farmer-preachers entered this tragic scenario during the summer of 1934. Meeting secretly at Tyronza, Arkansas (due west of Memphis), they founded the biracial Southern Tenant Farmers' Union (STFU). H. L. Mitchell, one of the white Socialists and a cofounder, claimed the union ultimately numbered as many as twenty-five thousand, spreading northward into the Missouri Bootheel, eastward into western Tennessee, into Mississippi, and most successfully, into Oklahoma, where the union became triracial, acquiring militant Cherokee and Choctaw leaders. For a while, the ensemble took on a dreamlike movement culture, with interracial conventions and picnics and stirring anthems composed and sung by black union troubadours. STFU members understood that the old system of tenancy was fast dissolving, and they behaved as a modern union. They called two cotton pickers' strikes; the one in 1936 seems to have succeeded in raising wages. On through the late-1930s, however, the STFU was drained by mounting evictions and out-migration of its membership. Few could afford modest dues. The Communist Party, always a rival for leadership of embattled workers, encouraged several gifted, separatist black leaders. The union split in 1939, then, for all practical purposes, dissolved.[28]

The STFU's movement culture, an ingenious synthesis of evangelical protestantism and socialist idealism, was glue insufficient to maintain the union's coherence. Its leadership, so carefully balanced by race, usually worked in harmony. But racial tensions at the grassroots compounded the destructive mischief of landlords, their law enforcement allies, and obtuse New Dealers. H. L. Mitchell, a man of sweetly generous disposition, always minimized color-consciousness and distrust among his followers. My own reading of the STFU's vast archive (a collection Mitchell, to his everlasting credit, preserved) leads to a compelling contrary conclusion: it was black members (a few separatists being exceptional) who were the STFU's principal interracialists and modern industrial unionists. They made most sacrifices of safety and offered most of the trust that was central to the union's culture and mission. Some white members—Mitchell, again, most noteworthy among them—overcame racist upbringings and the naïveté of frontierism and embraced color-blind unionism. Most whites, however, were comfortable only in tiny, all-white union locals. They never overcame racism. But I suspect there is more to their recalcitrance. They had seen northeastern Arkansas as another frontier of opportunity—now gone wrong, to be sure—but a frontier, nonetheless, where ultimately they might rediscover a life apart from the rest of the world. Unlike blacks, who had been hierarchical negotiators for generations, whites had little historical preparation for the difficult role of class struggle.[29]

So it was, too, in California, Illinois, Ohio, Michigan, Pennsylvania, and other places north, where millions of southern whites migrated, especially during the 1940s and 1950s. Occasionally progressive, they were much more often scabs, reluctant members of CIO unions at best, in urban industrial settings.[30] In the meantime, the rural South was transformed at last; the vice closed.

First, the dynamic of modern agronomy was finally realized in the South—the last American region to mechanize agriculture, or what remained of it. Cotton culture shrank to a cluster of counties in the lower Mississippi Valley and Texas. (California became the nation's cotton belt, Fresno the principal market.) The great hordes of mostly black mule-plowmen, hoers, and pickers who had serviced the old cotton culture were gone—to Chicago and Detroit and countless other cities across the nation. Thousands of mostly white-owned and operated little fruit and vegetable farms, from the valleys of Appalachia to the Gulf, disappeared, too, by the end of the 1950s, victims also of Californians' salubrious climate and their mastery of production and distribution to new supermarket chains. And most important, by 1959 there was not a single southern county classifiable as self-sufficient. What was left of the southern rural population, instead, included the United States' largest aggregation of poor people, and—a little-recognized statistic—most of them were white.[31]

The process of modernization had been protracted and traumatic, but now, for better or worse, southerners lived and labored in a new world, a "modern" one in the profound senses that virtually all production was specialized, and virtually everyone lived by cash exchanges. Retro eastern frontiers were at long last gone, and with them disappeared the traditional white dream of independence through modest material requirements and resourceful versatility. A shame, I think; and because modernization appeared so *recently* in so much of the region, memory of the old ways survives among those past fifty, who undoubtedly communicate aspects of the dream, at least, to the young. I suspect the dream lives on particularly among the contemporary rural poor, and among men called "rednecks," who may live in the country, the working-class suburbs, or the sprawling new cities themselves.

But meanwhile, the triumph of modern agronomy in the rural South played a role in reconfiguring the now-depopulated countryside. The Southeast is second only to the irrigated West in corporate or corporate-style farms. Machines permitted the recentralization of farming operations previously divided among tenants. Specialization and national competition (especially with the West) have meant a vast shrinkage of cultivated farmland across the South, too. (Machines and especially chemicals permit more production from less land.) Abandoned fields have returned to forests. The region has "greened," in the usage of a recent historian,[32] but it has been a greening of a precious sort. In fact, the South has become plantation country again, more so than in the high age of cotton culture. This time the plantations are loblollies. An ordered pine kingdom was long and difficult of creation, however—another development recent enough for living memory.

Progressive-era and 1920s professional forestry, governmental and corporate, probably had little effect upon most rural folk. Many of them labored part- or full-time in lumber camps and sawmills, but neither states nor counties had sufficient money (or, perhaps, political will) to enforce laws against fire. Nor were there many watchtowers or fire roads in forests. All this awaited the Great Depression and massive federal intrusions—and capital infusions—into the most remote hinterlands of the nation. The Civilian Conservation Corps (CCC), especially, initiated modern fire suppression. CCC workers constructed the towers and roads, often on state and private property, as well as in national forests. The federal government also undertook mass education in fire suppression, in league with state forest bureaus and professional foresters' groups—"Smokey the Bear" and "Keep Green" campaigns persisted long after the CCC's demise.[33]

It was during the 1930s, too, that the ingenious Dr. Charles Herty, a Georgia chemist, conducted laboratory work of revolutionary import for the South. Already famous for his contributions to the turpentine industry, during the Depression Herty demonstrated that young southern pines were essentially free of resin and an excellent (and cheaper) material for the making of paper. In Herty's time, virtually all newsprint and fine white paper in the United States was manufactured from Canadian spruce. Southern pine, it was assumed, was good only for lumber or, at best, the making of "kraft" (German and Swedish for "strong") materials, such as cardboard for boxing. In 1913 an Ohio papermaker had established a pulpmill for kraft at West Point, Virginia, near Williamsburg. During the twenties, the West Point mill, now an independent concern called the Chesapeake Corporation, undertook kraft papermaking on its own and began to acquire vast pine woodland reserves. Herty predicted that papermaking of all sorts— not only kraft but also newsprint and fine papers—would come to the source of undervalued southern pines. Herty, like many southern-born foresters, was a southern chauvinist: corporate pulp- and papermaking would rescue the region from its economic colonial bondage.[34]

Herty's prediction was technically correct but dubious in terms of political economy and rather long in implementation. It was not until after about 1960 that papermaking shifted from Canada and the United States' Pacific Northwest to the Southeast. Smaller, locally owned and managed mills such as Chesapeake Corporation and Camp Manufacturing of Franklin, Virginia, would not dominate this new "southern" business, either, but rather, established international giants headquartered in New York City, Portland, Oregon, and elsewhere. All the papermakers were troubled, however, by an ecological management challenge in southern forests; their solution, worked out during the 1950s and 1960s, placed the corporations in conflict with ordinary rural folk and outdoorsmen.

The problem was that over much of the South, pines were never the "natural climax" tree. It had only *seemed* so, because for three centuries, so long as farmers abandoned farmland, then reburned it twenty or thirty years later, deciduous competition with pines was destroyed. Then came the great pine cut-downs of the beginning of the twentieth century, then modern forestry's proscription of fire. Natural succession, uninterrupted by folk agronomy, transpired. By midcentury, government and corporate foresters in the South worried aloud and in print about a "hardwood menace." Both lumber and especially pulp and paper interests required pine monoculture. How to maintain pines, then?[35] It was a fine irony. A preliminary solution required foresters to modify their first canon. Pines resist fire, which destroys deciduous competition. So carefully "controlled burns" on would-be pine plantations were carefully introduced during the 1950s. Soon, however, the chemical wonders that were then accelerating the agricultural "Green Revolution" came to the rescue. DDT killed pests in woodlands plantations about as effectively as in food crops. More important, the devastating herbicides 2,4-D and 2,4,5-T, sprayed from ground or air, accomplished for the corporations the weed-free environment farmers came to take virtually for granted. Pine plantations, almost natural to coastal plains, might be extended through the piedmonts into the mountains themselves. The high cost of chemical maintenance of pine monoculture, meanwhile, meant that the largest companies would come to dominate the southern countryside. The high cost of monoculture also alienated small woodlot owners from modern forestry; and there ensued a mounting conflict between corporate owners and citizens accustomed to using forests for recreation and, even late in the twentieth century, as an open range for livestock. The federal Environmental Protection Agency's banning first of DDT, then during the early 1970s, of the herbicidal agents 2,4-D and 2,4,5-T, was inconvenient but hardly disturbing to the new structure of the rural South. A new commercial herbicide, also from agriculture, called "Roundup," did about as well.[36]

$\mathcal{P}$rofessional foresters had understood from the beginning the enormous scope of their problems: most of the nation's woodlands, especially in the East, were owned privately in small acreages—difficult to manage. And that southerners were prone to burn forests for a variety of quaint folkish reasons—a challenge to public education. Following the organization of enormous public forest reserves and institution of New Deal conservationism, however, a new reason for woods arson became apparent to the dullest experts: employment in hard times. Foresters had sought familiarity with locals in their communities, in hopes of discouraging arsonists. Then when fires broke out, usually but not always from lightning, they hired local men to fight them. The error in the method was discovered in the Jefferson National Forest in Virginia— and probably other places—during the 1930s: locals began to predict fires in the federal woodlands, then make themselves available as firefighters at the federal wage of 75 cents. Virginia's government paid 50 cents to extinguish blazes in state-owned forests; unsurprisingly, there were hardly ever fires in those forests.[37] Poor people remained resourceful.

The phenomenon provoked a scholarly study of southerners' pyromaniacal behavior in 1936, by one John P. Shea of the U.S. Forest Service. Allowing for Shea's middle-class professional biases, his conclusions remain a shocking trivialization of southern incendiaries' motivation. Fire setters lived in environments of "low stimulation," Shea observed, so they "craved excitement." Forest fires served merely this end. Forest conservationists' task was to locate alternative amusements for the bored ignorati.[38]

During World War II, forest arson subsided almost to insignificance. Governments and organized foresters declared the crime "tantamount to sabotage" by the enemy, and patriotism may indeed have changed southern behavior—for a while.[39] Perhaps just as likely, poor people found plenty of wartime work at better than federal firefighting wages. But about a decade after the war, amid the continuing catastrophic displacement of millions of rural folk and the early institution of the corporate system of managed forests, southerners were back to their old ways with a vengeance. At least this is what professional foresters, who produce fire statistics, maintained during the mid-1950s and long afterward. In 1956, about twelve hundred "citizens" attended the Southern Forest Fire Prevention Conference, hosted by the federal Forest Service's experiment station of New Orleans. Years later, early in 1986, a writer for *American Forests* (the popular journal of the American Forestry Association, whose members include foresters and the wood products industry as well as upper- and middle-class recreationists) dated "the growing arson epidemic" from approximately the same time as the Conference![40]

The lamented Hank Williams Sr. had been dead for three years in 1956. Yet millions still listened to his joyous composition celebrating the southern incendiary tradition, "Settin' the Woods On Fire." I did, as a boy; yet I can hardly suggest a causative relationship between Williams and persisting forest arson. Still, there may be other historical causes for an "epidemic" beginning during the fifties. This was, after all, the decade when corporate "third growth" forests matured under chemical and refined scientific management. In Virginia's Dismal Swamp, for example, the Camp Manufacturing Company settled a long boundary dispute with a corporate neighbor about 1952–53. Property lines finally established—and Camp on the brink of its merger with Union Bag—the company set about "get[ting] the hunting established so that we would have everything organized in hunting clubs[,] who in turn would be responsible for fire control," in the words of Jack Camp, corporate president. Camp had not included local working-class men in the combination hunting club/fire patrol, however, and one of them threatened a corporate attorney: "Look," the man said, "don't bother me about hunting. I hunted here, and my father and my sons, and we're gon' hunt here as long as we want to hunt here. You can forget trying to tell us what not to do." Years later, Jack Camp reflected upon "how rugged a lot of the people were around the edge of the Swamp. If people got upset with you, they'd set your woods on fire. That was their retaliation, you couldn't catch 'em. . . . Boy, once they get something against you, they'll burn your woods, or shoot you, or something like that. Pretty tough crowd."[41]

A host of the New Orleans conclave himself documented the "epidemic" in a 1981 issue of *American Forests*. In 1956 there were fifty-five thousand forest fires in the South; 1981 brought seventy-six thousand, an increase of thirty-eight percent. Better suppression reduced actual acres burned, but the far greater incidence of fires, especially those apparently set intentionally, was profoundly troubling. By the 1970s, after all, the poorest rural folk owned automobiles and television sets. Isolation and low environmental stimuli would no longer do, even for the forest intelligentsia, as an explanation for incendiarism.[42]

So during the 1970s two more scholars, Alvin L. Bertrand and Andrew W. Baird, conducted another study. Constrained by a small pool of informants—arsonists are not often apprehended and are seldom convicted when caught—Bertrand and Baird nonetheless developed what seems a credible set of motivations. First was traditional folk aesthetics: the sight, sound, and smell of burning woods *pleased* many people (men, women, and children). And forests with underbrush burned away *looked better,* "cleaner," to them. Second was comfort and safety: burning killed and/or deterred snakes, varmints, and insects. Third was a surprising persistence of the open range: poor folks unwilling (more likely, unable) to raise or buy feed for cattle, burned other property owners' woods in order to admit sunlight and induce pasture grass for free-ranging cows and steers. And fourth, revenge, a large category of behaviors both traditional and very modern: quarreling neighbors fired each others' woods. Hunters resentful of exclusion from forests now posted by clubs protested with the torch. Squirrel hunters resented pine monoculturists' killing of nut-bearing deciduous trees. From Livingston Parish, Louisiana, long a haven for arsonists, there appeared during the 1950s a ditty sung to a popular tune: "You've got the money / We've got the time / You deaden the hardwoods / And we'll burn the pine." Others attacked national forests out of resentment for Forest Service policies. And yet more arsonists had employment grievances against wood products companies. During the 1970s, for instance, three men set thirty-six fires around Drip Rock, Kentucky, when a tree-planting firm declined to rehire them for another year. And two Florida women spent

The Countercultural South

54

a day setting fires on the plantations of a paper company that would not give jobs to their sons. Bertrand and Baird's model "community" harboring such people was formally ill-educated, disliked foresters, open-ranged livestock, and professed "identification with lower social classes."[43]

Statistically, their model would most likely be situated in Louisiana. For according to the Forest Service, between 1974 and 1978 there were no fewer than 5,195 woods arsons there. Other Gulf States followed: Mississippi, 4,388; Alabama, 3,602. Georgia had 3,575 arsons; South Carolina, 2,554. The Sabine River must be the western border for forest arsonists, since Texas had only 425 cases. The Upper South, too, was less a concern for foresters. Virginia had only 400 arsons. The distribution of arsons seems less a matter of latitude and longitude, however, than rural poverty. For the Forest Service's data correlate well with the Southern Regional Council maps of Dixie's enormous "po' country."[44]

Nineteen eighty-five was a terrible forest-fire year: a deep January freeze, then drought and high winds to fuel and drive wildfires that leveled a quarter-million acres in the South. In the blackened aftermath, investigators classified no fewer than 60 percent of the conflagrations as arson. This *année horrible* climaxed a three-year holocaust, in which 224,549 fires burned more than five and a half million acres in the region. Lightning and humans' careless debris-burning apparently accounted for most of the disaster. But by 1985—another breathtaking statistic—almost 98 percent of all American forest arson took place in the Southeast.[45]

By this late date, the Forest Service had been obliged by circumstances to ally itself with a new, but burgeoning, federal bureau, the Drug Enforcement Agency. Another cause of woods arson had arisen. In Florida, drug dealers set signal fires to guide delivery planes; sometimes the fires got out of control. More significant, across the nation cultivators of cannabis took to the woods, and rivals not infrequently burned each other out. A map in *American Forests* prepared from DEA data reveals that arboreal marijuana planting is most common

Retro Frontiersmen

55

in regions with the most widespread rural poverty—the desert Southwest, Pacific Northwest, the northern Great Lakes, and of course, the Southeast, especially Appalachia and Ozarkia. It seems an updated but very old story, for here was (and remains) the landscape of the moonshiner, too, before, during, and since Prohibition.[46]

So frontiers persist, perhaps always will. A hegemonic culture—bourgeois or whatever—is just that, hegemonic, not total. All of them define and attempt to enforce laws, extending to everyone preferred behaviors—or else. But in rural America, notably the Southeast and especially its most impoverished subregions, illegal countercultural behavior is sufficiently furtive to elude most punishments. Too, this behavior eludes careful examination. Who, exactly, are these people who set the woods on fire? I have only correlated: they seem to be overwhelmingly white, working-class or poor, primarily southern men (with supportive women it would seem), who work, and like especially to play, outside. Excluded from privilege in an increasingly managed landscape, they break laws and inflict damage. I cannot accomplish much more description, social-scientifically, for my subjects have good reason to remain elusive.

There is more, however, because these white southerners are prominent in literature and popular culture. They are "crackers," "hillbillies," and especially "rednecks"—all pejoratives bestowed by representatives of a long succession of southern hegemonies, then consumed and broadcast by Yankees who share hegemonic understanding and control communications media. This is a subject appropriate (at the very least) to another, concluding, chapter.

"Redneck" Discourse

The Distemper of Laziness seizes the Men oftener much than the Women. These last Spin, weave and knit, all with their own hands, while their Husbands, depending on the Bounty of the Climate, are Sloathful in every thing but getting of Children, and in that only Instance make themselves useful Members of an Infant-Colony.
—William Byrd II on North Carolinians, 1728

When we got to the rural town late that night, it seemed desolate. . . . Just like on television, the only establishment open . . . was a saloon. It was filled with rednecks, rough, leather-skinned cats in cowboy hats, boots, and wide belts. My partner . . . took one peek inside and . . . stopped me in my tracks.
—Nathan McCall in Georgia, ca. 1985

How many hillbillies does it take to go possum hunting? Two, of course— one to get the possum and one to watch for oncoming traffic.
—Pat Furguson, 1994

I have found that anything that comes out of the South is going to be called grotesque by the northern reader, unless it is grotesque, in which case it is going to be called realistic.
—Flannery O'Connor

V. S. Naipaul, innocent intruder upon the complex southern business of social class and language, was made to understand that " 'redneck' " refers to a rural working man—that is, "The back of the man's neck is red from the sun." Then came a historical hypothesis: Naipaul "heard from an old Mississippian" that "when he was a child," " 'redneck' . . . was not a pejorative; was the opposite, in fact, and meant a man who lived by the sweat of his brow; *and that it was only in the 1950s, when the frontier or pioneer life was changing, that the word began to have unflattering associations.*"[1] The concept of the frontier emerges again, plus the notion that the South's very late "modernization" suddenly placed the rural working classes and poor on the defensive.

The hypothesis has appeal, sequencing causally the mechanization of agriculture—the appearance of the cotton harvester equipped with stereo and air-conditioner—with the passage into antiquity of mules and their sunburned drivers, during the 1950s and 1960s.[2] In 1951, the historian Albert D. Kirwan had entitled his best book, a saga of the political triumph of Mississippi's common white men, about the turn of this century, *Revolt of the Rednecks*.[3] Ironic timing, then, since the triumph began to turn to dust even as the volume appeared.

Or, the coincidence signifies nothing at all. Naipaul's hypothesis—via the "old Mississippian"—was in fact wrong as a generalization. "Rednecks" have *never* got respect from outsiders. The substance of Kirwan's book, and those of other liberal white southern writers born before 1925—C. Vann Woodward, W. J. Cash, Vernon Wharton, V. O. Key, and George Tindall—convey instead a long-standing and problematic negativity in portraiture of common white folks.[4] On "redneck" rouser James K. Vardaman's 1907 campaign for the U.S. Senate, for instance, Kirwan quoted a *Washington Post* correspondent's put-down of Vardaman's oratory: "His eloquence tells [only] with the rednecks and hill billies," that is, the easily gulled, the uneducated and meanspirited.[5] And the scholars, themselves, most children of Vardaman's zenith, could not escape the embarrassment of "rednecks'" backwardness and racism. "Rednecks" and "hillbillies" were, indeed, the problem of the South. The liberal explanation of social pathology was of course environmental: economic colonialism and poverty. So the logic of the forties, fifties, and sixties was to modernize and to conquer ignorance and poverty, and commoners of both the region's principal racial groups will behave rationally. Pejoratives would disappear with antique pathos and social types.[6]

Liberal logic (or dreaming) died hard. In 1987 the political scientists Earl and Merle Black finally documented the fallacy, the failure of liberal assumptions, beyond dispute. The South had industrialized—farms, towns, and cities alike; schooling was universalized; a civil rights movement had undone Jim Crow. Yet racial suspicion and hostility remained the rule; whites and blacks with the same class interests seldom voted together or cooperated. Neo-Vardamans thrived—only now (curiously) more often as Republicans than Democrats.[7] And at the end of the century, "redneck," "hillbilly," and other pejoratives assumed, if anything, greater currency and intensity.

A doleful development. One prays, retrospectively, that liberal logic had been sound. Or, prospectively, that it might yet prevail; for thirty years (i.e., since integration and relative prosperity began) may not be enough time to right so many decades of suffering and wrong. The previous two chapters sought to explain deep historical roots for the races' persistent divergence. This last one returns to white classes and the nearly ageless (not merely the post-1950)—and perversely one-sided—discourse on "redneck" pathology. My objective, naturally, is a discourse that is not perverse.

$\mathcal{B}$etween the late-1930s and mid-1970s, university presses published three substantial monographs on southern poor whites in literature, and scholars still fill journals with critical analyses of individual writers on "rednecks," especially Faulkner.[8] Both the literature and its interpretation are appallingly vague to social scientists and historians, however. For although "poor whites" appears in two of the book-length treatments ("folk" in the third), the literary tradition often includes independent property-holders—the yeomanry, mountain herdspeople, and those who subsisted in the coastal piney woods. The vagueness—the ignorance—is owing to the sources of the literature. They are invariably formally educated, privileged men.

William Byrd II was their archetype. A lawyer, merchant, slaveholder and planter, the founder of Richmond, and possessor of a library of four thousand volumes and a billiard room, Byrd—traversing the fringes of the Dismal Swamp during late-1720s—encountered countercultural white people. That they had little he might have tolerated. But that they seemed not to *want* more was intolerable. So Byrd is credited with the invention of white ethnic put-downs in North America, an infinitely adaptable formula—the same as "Polish" jokes in the twentieth-century Middle West. A Carolinian, then, in Byrd's usage became a "Lubber"—lazy and stupid, living upon nature. The swamps sheltered free-range hogs; believing that excessive pork consumption induced extreme cases of scurvy, then yaws, causing degeneration of noses, Byrd joked that "after three good Pork years, a Motion had like to have been made in the [North Carolina] House of Burgesses, that a Man with a Nose shou'd be incapable of holding any Place of Profit in the Province."[9]

William Byrd's humor was hardly known for more than a century, however, until Edmund Ruffin printed the *History of the Dividing Line* in his agricultural journal, the *Farmers' Register*, in 1841. Ruffin discovered Byrd's manuscripts in possession of James River neighbors, descendants of Byrd, who agreed to the dissemination of the eighteenth-century documents among Ruffin's genteel subscribers and fellow members of the Historical and Philosophical Society of Virginia.[10] The timing corresponds to the real emergence of the "redneck" genre. Six years before Ruffin published Byrd, A. B. Longstreet's collection of backwoods picaresques, *Georgia Scenes*, appeared. Longstreet, a Yale-educated attorney, editor, businessman, preacher, and college president, introduced to a huge audience—there were eleven editions of *Georgia Scenes* before the end of the century—stout, loutish, violent frontier southern white men. Especially in a story called "The Fight," and in another, "The Gander Pulling," Longstreet demonstrated with more enduring cleverness than de Tocqueville the horrors of (white) democracy. (Longstreet was a Calhounite, then a Whig.) It was in "The Fight" that readers met the character Ransy Sniffle, prototype to virtually every inhabitant of every tobacco road from that day to this: Sniffle was, wrote Longstreet, "a sprout of Richmond who, in his earlier days, had fed copiously upon red clay and blackberries." The result was "a complexion that a corpse would have disdained to own, and an abdominal rotundity that was quite unprepossessing." Sniffle's "shoulders were fleshless and elevated; his head large and flat, his neck slim and translucent; and his arms, hands, fingers, and feet were lengthened out of all proportion to the rest of his frame. . . . His height was just five feet nothing; and his average weight in blackberry season, ninety-five." [11]

Davy Crockett's *Autobiography,* Joseph G. Baldwin's *Flush Times of Alabama and Mississippi,* and George W. Harris's "Sut Lovingood" sketches, among other late-antebellum classics, elaborated the genre and its typology. The corpus entire is much valued by literary historians and much reprinted and introduced. And reasonably so, of course. Here is an "American" mode—frontier humor—with long proverbial legs. The least perceptive students will discover in Longstreet and Baldwin, especially, intimations of Twain, Faulkner, Caldwell, and O'Connor.[12] The intrinsic value of these nineteenth-century works I eagerly acknowledge. Clever, evocative wit, and distracting entertainment are no small achievements. But reading Longstreet and Crockett, for example, seems impossible without evoking social history, too—that is, presumed objective "truth." So I suggest that these pioneers of American humor should also be read as insidiously biased field anthropologists. They were, like early professionals in more distant "primitive" regions, imperial. The writers were creatures of presumption, representatives of the market of print, of print's privileged audience. They were not voices *of* their subjects, but condescending ones.[13]

At the very end of the nineteenth century, there finally appeared a sympathetic voice in the unlikely person of young

Ellen Glasgow. The daughter of one of Richmond's premier families, heiress to the big house at One West Main Street, Glasgow set out to write a fictional social history of Virginia since the Civil War. While her elder contemporaries—Thomas Nelson Page most famous among them—featured plantations, the white aristocracy, faithful slaves, the Confederate dead, and Reconstruction in their work, Glasgow wrote about ordinary white people and their problems. From *The Descendant* (1897) through *The Voice of the People* (1900), *The Deliverance* (1904), *The Miller of Old Church* (1911), and her penultimate novel, *Barren Ground* (1925), Glasgow recounted with sympathy and remarkable accuracy the travails and triumphs of the yeomanry and "trash"—their reconstruction of destroyed farms, their defiance of the Old Dominion's burdensome elite traditions, their wars with creditors and railroads, their political ascent to authority as Populists. Glasgow was most responsible for creating a critical realism that briefly dominated the literature of the South, during the 1920s and early 1930s.[14]

The post–World War I collapse of agricultural commodity prices and the onset of depression in farm country no doubt prompted the spate of socially engaged fiction, written often by authors from humble rural circumstances. The southern version is remembered as "sharecropper realism," and began with the appearance of Edith Summers Kelly's *Weeds* in 1923. Here the spunky spirit and high hopes of a Kentucky girl are broken after her marriage to a luckless tobacco tenant. The last and best known was Henry Kroll's *Cabin in the Cotton* (1931), which was made into a 1932 film of the same name, starring the youthful Bette Davis in her first Dixie bitch role ("I'd love to kiss you, but I just washed my hair").[15]

In a sense, if one is very generous, Erskine Caldwell continued critical realism during the 1930s and later, as he surmounted the heights of best-sellerdom. Caldwell was the son of a progressive minister who taught him sympathy for the downtrodden. Erskine became a left New Dealer, and there are passages in Caldwell's novels—especially the first two, *Tobacco Road* (1932) and *God's Little Acre* (1933)—with clinical detail of the rural South's pathology, resembling some of the best Chapel Hill sociology of the period. Ultimately, though, redeeming social value and sympathy are hard to find in an American Rabelais. For Caldwell reintroduced humor into "redneck" portraiture, not merely the humor of Longstreet, Baldwin, and company, but twentieth-century "Freudian" humor. Caldwell's memorable characters are dominated by "animal instincts," rendering the writer more a naturalist than a realist, as some critics have insisted. They also find in Caldwell's human creatures an ennobling connectedness to the land, to the natural setting: Jeeter Lester *must* farm, and Ty-Ty Walden's last name is heavy-handedly symbolic of Caldwell's larger purpose. The writer's real social criticism, then, becomes his mockery not of his own characters but of an American Dream that honest, willing people can make a living at farming. So much for generous criticism. Caldwell disarmingly revealed his main purpose in his principal autobiography: he was a hungry, ambitious young man searching for a manner of writing that would sell well. The depravity of the rural poor worked. His was a naturalism, if one will, of the creative goad.[16]

For her part, Ellen Glasgow despaired. Caldwell, William Faulkner, and T. S. Stribling had founded, she wrote in 1935, a "Southern Gothic School." "What is left of the pattern? Has Southern life—or is it only Southern fiction—become one vast disordered sensibility?"[17] A much younger white southerner, and a follower of H. L. Mencken at that, agreed with Glasgow, more or less. "Growing steadily more realistic," wrote W. J. Cash in 1941, "the Caldwells and the Faulkners, sternly rooting out not only sentimentality but even sentiment . . . remained in some curious fashion romantics in their choice of materials—shall we say, romantics of the appalling."[18]

Cash's susceptibility to the word "realistic" suggests the maddening problem of audience that Flannery O'Connor would immortalize later: "anything that comes out of the South is going to be called grotesque by the northern reader, unless it is grotesque, in which case it is going to be called realistic." O'Connor, who earned some acclaim as a creator of grotesques, herself, during the 1950s and early 1960s, was impatient with and ultimately indifferent to readers' simplemindedness. She had, in her own words, "other fish to fry"— namely, her confrontation with a generation who believed "God is dead." [19] So O'Connor is properly read as a Catholic writer preoccupied with grace in a world of secular intellectual pretension and theological tomfoolery. Still, one must wonder why, then, O'Connor—a woman of privilege and a Catholic who happened to live in rural Georgia—chose Protestant working-class and poor whites as comic subjects. Did she find her own social class inadequate to demonstrate human yearning, irrationality, and the necessity of grace? Is she without responsibility for reasonably intelligent readers' social-historical conclusions from reading, say, "A Good Man Is Hard to Find," and "Good Country People"? [20] It is not an easy or trivial question. A mere pedestrian scribbler, myself, I have experienced seemingly willful misreadings; yet I think authors *at least* share with readers such responsibility. In O'Connor's case, the audience has not been large, nor mischief widespread beyond critical circles and literature classrooms. Her fellow Georgian, Erskine Caldwell, however, had (and seems to retain) an enormous audience, and committed much mischief.

Unless John Grisham surpassed Caldwell while I hunched over a keyboard in my garret, Caldwell remains the bestselling author of southern fiction, of all time. (I do not forget Margaret Mitchell. Caldwell wrote more books, and *Tobacco Road* had a long run on Broadway, too; it was also made into a movie, as was *God's Little Acre*.) Caldwell's intellect does not challenge and engage like O'Connor's. O'Connor was not without interest in selling her work, but she was never adrift and literally hungry, as the older writer was, during the late twenties and early thirties. Caldwell's confession to cynical opportunism in his 1951 autobiography should not be dismissed as more Caldwellian outrageousness. His behavior during the late thirties, at the height of his fame, documents the case. Worst, I think, was his picture-book project, *You Have Seen*

Their Faces (1937), with the famous photographer Margaret Bourke-White, who was then Caldwell's wife. They traveled about the disintegrating plantation South by car, Bourke-White in an expensive coat and worried about lighting, insinuating herself into black and white poor folks' church services, rearranging the interiors of their cabins. Caldwell offered to pay a couple for posing. Bourke-White reported that they declined cash, preferring snuff. "So far as we could tell," she wrote, "they hadn't any food. . . . They seem to live on snuff and religion." Finally, back home in New York City, Caldwell composed captions for Bourke-White's photos, placing quotation marks around them and leaving readers to conclude that these were the words of their humble subjects.[21] Such have been the servants and interpreters of the South's majority, "rednecks" and "blacknecks" alike.

In the academic and literary worlds, and perhaps far beyond, the most devastating portraiture of common white folks came in two books published by Knopf in 1941: W. J. Cash's *Mind of the South* and William Alexander Percy's *Lanterns on the Levee*. Born in 1900, Cash was the son of a sometime cotton mill foreman, but relatives were millhands and farmers. He was, conceivably, far enough removed from the region's upper classes to disdain them, yet close enough to the poor both to sympathize with and fear them. That he anguished over his portraiture is legendary. (*Mind of the South* was a dozen years in the making, and Cash's suicide not long after publication was not unconnected to his tortured quandries over his own people.) I daresay, however, that Cash's "savage ideal"—the most memorable of his generalizations about southern history and culture—legitimated an old popular conviction that poor whites were the embodiment of southern intolerance. H. L. Mencken had declared this flatly, a generation before. Now, in Cash's compelling prose, frustrated rustics were prohibitionists (albeit frequently drunk), antimodernists, and antievolutionists, and constituted one hundred percent of every lynch mob—spiritual kin to their contemporaries in Hitler's Germany.[22]

William Alexander Percy anguished over neither class nor race. He was a Mississippi Delta lawyer, businessman, planter, poet, and critic—a man utterly comfortable with everything but time. This had passed by his class and their finer sensibilities, notably charity and other responsibilities of paternalism. *Lanterns on the Levee* was subtitled *Recollections of a Planter's Son,* and William Alexander's father, LeRoy Percy, figures large as beloved "*père,*" dutiful planter, honorable statesman, and exemplar of *temps perdu.* What was lost was a way of life, most emphatically during the U.S. senatorial contest of 1911, which the elder Percy lost to James K. Vardaman. In the aftermath, young Percy observed a Vardaman supporter—"An old man wet with tobacco juice and furtive-eyed"—who, as Percy reported, "summed up the result: 'Wal, the bottom rail's on top and it's gwiner stay thar.'" Percy thought the man "wasn't much as a human being, but as a diagnostician and prophet he was first-rate. It was my first sight of the rise of the masses, but not my last. Now we have Russia and Germany, we have the insolence of organized labor and the insolence of capital, both examples of the insolence of the parvenu. . . . The herd is on the march, and when it stampedes, there's blood galore and beauty is china under its hoofs."[23]

Young Percy was prepared for this doleful, almost Cash-like summary by a campaign confrontation with Vardamanites. "I looked over the ill-dressed, surly audience, unintelligent and slinking," he wrote. "They were the sort of people that lynch Negroes, that mistake hoodlumism for wit, and cunning for intelligence, that attend revivals and fight and fornicate in the bushes afterward. They were undiluted Anglo-Saxons. They were the sovereign voter. It was so horrible it seemed unreal." Democracy's cataclysm of 1911 led Percy finally to generalize on "The poor whites of the South: a nice study in heredity and environment. Who can trace their origins," he wondered, or "estimate their qualities, do them justice? Not I." But in fact he could. "The present breed is probably the most unprepossessing on the broad face of the ill-populated earth. I know they are responsible for the only American ballads, for camp meetings, for a whole new and excellent school of Southern literature. I can forgive them as the Lord forgives, but admire them, trust them, love them—never."[24] For my part, I can respect William Alexander Percy's forthrightness, grateful that he never presumed to write popular fiction about people he despised. Percy may deserve some credit, too, that the fiction of his adoring kinsman (and adoptive son), Walker Percy, is intellectually profound, as Catholic as O'Connor's, and so preoccupied with the angst of the privileged that it largely ignores the masses.[25]

The elder Percy's 1941 diatribes, and the problems of authorial voice and audience, nonetheless survive. So who speaks authoritatively for ordinary southern white folks? The literary canon, recently expanded to include women and black southerners, remains effectively imperial, with little hope for accommodation of new voices. In 1994, for instance, the Louisiana State University Press announced a new series called "Voices of the South." It will not publish new authors but republish old: Fred Chappell, George Garrett, Peter Taylor, Ellen Douglas, and others, in 1994; Robert Penn Warren and Erskine Caldwell later. The University of Georgia Press, meanwhile, announced early in 1994 that it was undertaking "new editions of Erskine Caldwell's greatest works." *Tobacco Road* and *God's Little Acre* premiered, early in 1995; others are to follow. And the University of Mississippi thrives, of course, on William Faulkner and his works, conducting endless scholarly conferences on "Faulkner and. . . ."[26] One is obliged to search other media, then, for authoritative voices.

The most likely, the most obvious, place to look would be country music. Southerners black and white, literate and illiterate, have composed and performed music of many sorts. Before the commercialization of music by the recording industry and radio, during the 1920s, the music was called "folk" and "authentic," implying that business despoils the genuine. Yet for a long time, the music business accommodated poor rural and working-class composers, performers, and audiences. Quite logical, in "market" terms; for into the 1960s, anyway, country music's audience was primarily southern, and still in the throes of rural depopulation, mechanization, and urbanization known as "modernization." This is not to suggest that country music lyrics were coherent or class-conscious in a transparently political sense. The audience reflected a huge population in dramatically different topographies, crop cultures, industrial situations. Sometimes working people's lamentations identified the region's abstract unity in economic dependency—"Down on Penny's Farm," for instance, illustrating farm tenancy; and "Sixteen Tons," on mining coal for payment in company scrip. More often, country songs were sentimental evocations of specific places, family, romantic love, and moving. All these themes, especially the last, comment on the collapse of the remains of small-scale farming, familism, economic independence, and localism. Hank Williams Sr. was, arguably, the most ingenious and sweetly evocative of "redneck" troubadours during this protracted, difficult period of transition.[27]

By about 1970 the "modernization" of the rural South was more or less complete, Williams was long dead, and the country music audience was vastly transformed. The southern industrial working class was enlarged; and as we have already observed, the country population, while shrunken, still included the largest concentration of rural poor in the nation. But country music also became rather thoroughly nationalized, particularly during the 1980s and 1990s. Part of the nationalization was owing to the migration of four and a half million southern whites to the Northeast, Middle West, and West, where radio and television stations responded to demand. Part may also result from the stagnation of rock and roll music and the aging of the population: fringe rockers' unintelligible lyrics and runaway decibels compelled only the very young, while country composers' plain-talking sentiments and performers' (relatively) drugless style touched, then enveloped, the over-thirty bourgeoisie. By 1992 country was certifiably the most popular musical mode in the United States.[28]

For older fans and especially for slumming academic analysts, popularity is profoundly problematic: country has lost its identity as the music of the white southern folk. The complaint is an old one, raised against the first amplified instruments, and especially during the sixties against Chet Atkins' and other Nashville marketers' "uptown" sound, or conscious resort to pop. The late-1980s witnessed a "restoration" movement in the industry—that is, a revival of fiddles, quieter Dobros, and "adult" love themes conveyed in styles reminiscent of Ernest Tubb and the elder Williams. Randy Travis and Reba McEntire were its stars. But paradoxically, while Travis, McEntire, and other newcomers recollected the good old days, their ingenue charms and striking good looks—in concert and on television—tempted marketers in the direction of youth. For despite the passing of the great youth bulge in the American population, the immature remain the most important consumers of popular culture. According to the head of MCA records, "The driving demographics for the record industry are 15-to-25-year-olds—they are the ones who buy records," adding, "and they never used to listen to country before."[29] Country radio stations began to announce themselves as "Young Country"; graying but still lively singers disappeared. Country music became mall music. Early in 1994, driving on Richmond's Main Street, searching my dial for good radio, I nearly crashed into Ellen Glasgow's house when I heard the mellifluous baritone of Merle Haggard. By this time Reba McEntire had virtually crossed over to rock, bringing into question whether the new audience of youth were actually "country" music fans, after all.

Randy Travis, meanwhile, was eclipsed. Garth Brooks had become the new superstar, not only of country but, statistically, of American musical entertainment. Brooks's record distributor explained the simple ingredients of his popularity: "Garth is like Led Zeppelin meets Roy Rogers." That is, Brooks combines western attire, country music signatures, rock theatricality, and middle-class Oklahoma conventionality. Appropriately, Brooks appeared on the cover of *Forbes* magazine early in 1992. *Forbes* analysts thought the Brooks rage "suggests that American popular culture is taking a new, healthier direction." The music, especially in multiplying dance clubs, "is less solipsistic and drug oriented," they wrote. "Dancing becomes a social activity again. . . . The sexual electricity is there, but it isn't vulgar or violent." *Quel bourgeois!* Brooks is a most suitable spokesman, too. A marketing/advertising major in college, he declared with air-tight logic, "I believe in the Wal-Mart school of business." T-shirts sold at his concerts are "advertisement on someone's back," so he insisted that they be heavy, all-cotton, the best one could buy for the price. *Forbes* liked that, too: "Good quality at a reasonable price. What more can you ask from the entertainment industry—or any business?"[30] One is reminded of the more laconic Don Vito Corleone who, dismissing roots and old loyalties for advantage, said simply, "It's *business.*"

Manhattan, Don Vito's first American base, was the last outpost still resisting Young Country. So in May 1993, a Nashville consortium undertook a campaign into this heart of darkness. "Country Takes Manhattan" was billed as a ten-day festival, with venues at Radio City, Carnegie Hall, Beacon Theater, and Central Park. The executive director of the Country Music Association reasoned that "the music and the artists have changed a lot, and the product is probably more palatable to a lot of people." The Manhattan festival had its own executive director, and a corporate sponsor, Frito-Lay.[31] And so it goes.

Still, while choice narrows on radio bands and concert stages, the industry remains loose enough to support versions of "redneck" voices. Since the late-1960s, Merle Haggard and Dolly Parton, for instance, have consistently composed and sung songs about rural and working-class life, sometimes with an edge of class resentment. Haggard's "Mama Tried," "Hungry Eyes," "Roots of My Raisin'," "Okie from Muskogee," and "If We Make It to December" are bitterly so. Parton's "Coat of Many Colors" and "Chicken Every Sunday" are more sentimental, but the latter lectures the privileged, as does Parton's more recent hit, "Nine to Five." Tom T. Hall's "Harper Valley P.T.A." defended working people against bourgeois hypocrisy. Then, in 1973, Johnny Russell broke new ground with "Red Necks, White Sox, and Blue Ribbon Beer," a rowdy celebration of male working-class culture, contemptuous of "the white-collar crowd." The taboo against embracing a derogatory word now blasted, a flood of "redneck pride" songs followed. Best remembered are David Allen Coe's "Long Haired Redneck," Jerry Jeff Walker's "Redneck Mother," and Vernon Oxford's "Redneck! (The Redneck National Anthem)." During the 1980s Hank Williams Jr. extended the subgenre to militant regionalism and scary survivalism (notably with "A Country Boy Can Survive"), and Charlie Daniels, Willie Nelson, and Waylon Jennings celebrated the counterculturalism of "country boys," "cowboys," and "outlaws"—all cognates for "rednecks" and "hillbillies."[32] Thus was the way prepared for a revival of the industry's senior citizen, George Jones, late in 1993, with a hit entitled "High Tech Redneck." Jones hit the road early the following year with a "High Tech Redneck Tour."

What does this mean? The turning of pejoratives into badges of identity and pride is not an unknown phenomenon. Some African Americans—by no means all—call each other "niggers." This practice, however, is generally a *private* one, a comradely, affectionate exchange among brothers (it is a male thing)—never a proclamation inviting nonbrothers' usage. For ours is a hierarchical, intolerant world, one that neither compensates nor esteems all work, that fears nonconformity as dangerous to the vested order of things. The universality of class/regional pejoratives illustrates this. On the streets of northern Italian cities, for instance, natives disdainfully mutter "terroni" when working-class migrants from Campagna or Sicily come into view. (The word translates literally as "people of the earth," but its meaning is about the same as "nigger" or "redneck." What does disdain for people-of-the-earth convey about the disdainers?) And on the other side of the world, in southeastern Kalimantan (or "Borneo"), cosmopolitan Javanese call remote Meratus tribespeople "Bukit," the equivalent of "hillbillies." In Vietnam, Montagnards were (and perhaps remain) the lowest of low-class people. And in the remote Dinaric Alps, mountain communities of Herzegovinian Croats, Sandzak Muslims, and especially secessionist Serbs are today recognized as the most recalcitrant and fearsome of marginal people in the world. They are, according to a *New York Times* writer, "wild, warlike, frequently lawless societies whose feuds and folklore have been passed on to the present day." More yesterday's people. There is no affection in these usages, nor understanding, never sympathy.[33]

In America, public announcements of pride in lower-class identity are usually expressed *silently*—in the wearing of certain clothes, long hair on males (evoking another counterculture), the driving of pickup trucks. On the last, in the South and in some nonsouthern states, such as Indiana, one spies Confederate flag licenses and decals. The owners of such pickups in Indiana may or may not be descendants of southern migrants. (If so, ancestors were likely Unionists, anyway.) The descendants, meanwhile, resist righteous complaints about the Confederate flag's symbolism. To them, it signifies not the enslavement of black folks but resistance to condescending authority and to bourgeois conformity. The flag declares that "rednecks," "hillbillies," "country boys," "hicks," "cowboys," and "outlaws" are countercultural; they do not submit to national norms of work discipline and consumption. The rebel flag speaks plainly, "In your face, suit!" An outsider does not address such people as "redneck."

The silent language of the flag and other "redneck" signifiers is not, then, mere "lifestyle" display but serious social criticism. In his own way, V. S. Naipaul's loquacious Mississippi informant conveyed this meaning clearly enough. "I admire them for their independence," he declared. "But it's not right for the society now. No question about it. It was great a long time ago. But not now." Why not? Simply: "You can't get business done in a modern city with that kind of mentality. We got to change that redneck society"—and he added, portentously, "that black society," which also hindered modern urban efficiencies.[34]

The Nashvillian discourse in recent years, meanwhile, is far more problematical because it is so confused. Twenty years ago, Hugh Cherry, a reflective country music disc jockey, watched a sold-out Loretta Lynn concert in Oakland, California. Mindful of Lynn's eastern Kentucky origin and public persona, Cherry observed, "While being a 'hillbilly' was something you were born to and fated to remain in the 1930s, anyone who is a 'hillbilly' today is a 'hillbilly' by choice." Richard Peterson, an academic cultural critic, agrees. "To call oneself a redneck is not so much to *be* a redneck by birth or occupational fate," he wrote recently, "but rather to identify with an anti-bourgeois attitude and lifestyle."[35]

In other words, they suggest to us, consciousness determines being—the principal theoretical fallacy of Mao Tse Dong. (Marx thought the opposite—that socioeconomic being indicated consciousness.) The affluent capitalist expression of the fallacy makes our world go around: corporate designers create and offer to the affluent "lifestyles," which are really only patterns of consumption, to be adopted and discarded at will. Donned and shucked often enough, "lifestyles" keep stores in the malls busy, factories humming. So, be a middle-class suburbanite—minivan, suit on weekdays, J. Crew on weekends. Be a chic urban poet—public transportation, jeans and black turtleneck, pricey loft and exotic decor. Or, choose to be a "redneck" this year—pickup truck, baseball cap, boots and jeans, and (of course) Hank Williams Jr. in the CD-player. Authorial voices become market bites, successful advertising becomes life itself. George Jones, a man of humble, rural origin, should mind this. But it's only *bidnis.* So much for so-called country music.

*T*here is another medium, full of bytes of another kind, that has encompassed our subject. Among hundreds of computer subscriber networks is one called BUBBA-L, or "the Bubba line." "Bubba" is southern baby talk for "brother," all too often sticking to grown men. But "Bubba" has also come to mean about the same thing as "good ole boy," a drawling, unprepossessing white male, perhaps the same as a "redneck," but reputedly of gentler temperament. ("Redneck" is freighted with too many knives, shotguns, and ropes.) Yankee journalists apparently discovered Bubba in 1976, in Plains, Georgia, then rediscovered him in Little Rock more recently. That Bill Clinton was a Rhodes scholar and stellar Yale law student renders the appellation "Bubba Bill" not only oxymoronic but also transparently hostile.

Southern white *middle-class* men actually favor Bubba, however, according to sociologist John Shelton Reed, who describes the context for a late-twentieth-century crisis of identity in Dixie's suburban sprawls. Women and men adopt incompatible modes, conceivably explaining escalating divorce rates. But actual or potential marital disharmony is not so much Reed's subject as affluence, "lifestyle" choice, and the compelling persistence of old southern white social types. On virtually every bourgeois coffee table in botanical zone eight, *Southern Living* magazine illuminates an updated version of domestic feminine graciousness, à la Melanie Wilkes. Girls and women aspire to be "ladies," then. Boys and men, logically, should opt for "gentlemen," confidently surveying magnolia and crape myrtle from their piazzas, julep at hand. But "gentlemen," as Reed persuades, has fallen on awful times as a type. Ashley Wilkes, after all, was a wimp, dependent upon the kindness of women, ineffectual at business, unthinkable as a Jaycee. Suburban men understand that success in business requires ferocious competitiveness, teamwork, and affectionate buddyhood among teammates—something very much like football culture. They are fans, fonder of beer than juleps, of the sports pages than the book review. Reed's contemporary suburban southern male, then, has chosen Bubba as his beau ideal.[36]

Such men "speak" long distance to each other via BUBBA-L. So what do they say? In 1993, the subject was the identification of "rednecks"—"You may be a redneck if . . ." went the inquiry. The exercise was actually an exchange of humor of a particular sort. Although I am not a subscriber, a printout of the composite answer came to hand. The 109 one-liners are easily classifiable into two types. The first (by far the larger group) is class condescension, or correlations of ignorance, uncleanness, laziness, criminality, and low aesthetics with low income. Following is a small illustrative sample:

You may be a redneck if . . .
You ever cut your grass and found a car.
You own a home that is mobile and 5 cars that aren't.
You think the stock market has a fence around it.
You own a homemade fur coat.
You burn your yard rather than mow it.
Your wife's job requires her to wear an orange vest.
You hammer bottle caps into the frame of your front door to make it look nice.
You think a subdivision is part of a math problem.
You think a hot tub is a stolen bathroom fixture.
You consider your license plate personalized because your father made it.
You think Dom Perignon is a Mafia leader.
You actually know which kind of leaves make the best substitute for toilet paper.

And so on, revealing, I am persuaded, that Bubbas squirm uncomfortably in their hot tubs, oppressed by the never-ending expense and bother of monocultural lawns and all the other pretenses of life-as-seen in *Southern Living.* Interpretation of the other category I leave to psychoanalysts; this one encompasses sex, notably incest and bestiality:

> You may be a redneck if . . .
> Your family tree does not fork.
> You ever had to scratch your sister's name out of a
> message that begins, "For a good time call. . . ."
> Your brother-in-law is also your uncle.
> You view the upcoming family reunion as a chance to
> meet women.
> You've ever heard a sheep bleat and had romantic
> thoughts.[37]

So much for (faux) Bubba who, it turns out, is not so kind-hearted after all. He seems to me more insidious than the cosmopolites of Lombardy and Java. They at least do not attempt to consume the "terroni" and "Bukit" while disparaging them. So I return to the medium of print—to a literary canon I would expand to discover genuine voices of ordinary southern white folks. My list is brief; this is perhaps because I have not read everything, although I am beneficiary to literary mentors' guidance. But more probably because there are so few writers who even approximate my simple criteria: the first of these is negative—no cultural imperialists. A writer must accept her/his subjects on their own terms; cultural criticism will evoke and *explain,* not condescend. Nor will humor. Second, is a given with any canon. Works must have intrinsic worth—they will be complex, well written. Yet I value especially writers who capture the textured detail of specific places. There is *a* South, of course—that wonderful, awful abstraction by which some of us communicate and thrive. Mostly "South" is a pernicious abstraction, however—simplifying, blurring, slurring distinctions that are life itself. John Shelton Reed once demonstrated this point in a marvelous essay on the problem of sociology in the South. "Sociology," wrote Reed, "is a *generalizing* discipline. It requires, at least initially, that one ignore the differences between individuals and between groups, and concentrate upon what they have in common." This hardly ever resonates with southerners, who "insist on the sort of detail that social science" finds irrelevant. Southerners are "particularistic" rather than "universalistic," as witnessed by the narrative detail of country music lyrics, southern humor (which eschews one-liners for stories), and regional fiction.[38] That Reed's essay is collected in a volume entitled *One South*— Reed has larger fish to fry, not unlike Flannery O'Connor— should not diminish his lucid observation.

In academic critical circles, autobiography has lately acquired cachet. High time, for historians—notoriously sluggish at theory—have long recognized not only literary value but also a wealth of authentic detail in the medium. I recommend three southern white autobiographies. The first two instructed me during the 1980s, when I was writing a book about the modernization of southern agriculture and rural life. The last, a recent work, profoundly touched me as I labored at a study of rural landscape in southeastern Virginia and adjacent eastern North Carolina.

First, Harry Crews. Crews is an English professor famous for provocative essays and fiction evocative of Hemingway. He is a "man's" writer—of hard drinking, fighting, and blood sports—but not this man's favorite. Crews is also the author of a remarkable little memoir, however, called *A Childhood, The Biography of a Place*, first published in 1978.[39] Covering only the first six years of his life (the late-1930s and early-1940s), *Childhood* offers revelatory detail about life in Bacon County, in southeastern Georgia's sandy "piney-woods," at the end of the era of cotton, mule-power, and noncash exchanges. Crews's parents were small landowners who sometimes took on tenants and hired farmworkers. They hardly suited the image of southern landlords, however. Their home was a rude shack without a water supply indoors; they ate the plainest (but wholesomest) food and worked like driven slaves on their own acreage. After the parents divorced, Crews's mother was obliged to migrate to Jacksonville, Florida, where she found factory work. The very young Harry took up petty crime. Returning to Bacon County, they resumed a hard-scrabble existence. Bacon had no city; and virtually no one had a car, even during World War II. So the family (now including a stepfather) "lived at home," as the expression for self-sufficiency had it, raising and preserving their own vegetables and meat. It was a hard existence, but independent and, one must gauge, for Crews is no sentimentalist, rather satisfactory. One is struck especially by Crews's recollection of Bacon's social relations. Local and itinerant tenants and farm laborers were more folks. A black family were more like friends and neighbors than servants and clients—not that Bacon's whites were innocent of racism.

Memory's eccentricity is so often rewarding in its detail. Crews's recollections of mules, horses, the minutiae of farm life, are such. His boyhood preoccupation with humans' physical appearances seems especially so. Crews "became fascinated with the Sears catalogue," he writes, "because all the people in its pages were perfect." By contrast, "nearly everybody" he knew at the time "had something missing, a finger cut off, a toe split, an ear half-chewed away, an eye clouded with blindness from a glancing fence staple. And if they didn't have something missing, they were carrying scars from barbed wire, or knives, or fishhooks." His stepfather bore marks from human teeth on his cheek; later a hog nearly bit off a finger. Crews himself suffered burns over most of his body when, about age five, he fell into a hog-scalding cauldron.[40]

The subject evokes the grotesques of Dixie Gothic fiction, and (as I read him) Crews relishes a bit too much his boyhood discovery of the extent of disfigurement in his world. He does not quite tell us that Sears catalogue models were imperial, a beginning to the cultural intrusion of "normality," and a view of his own kind as something, perhaps Gothic, to write about later, conceivably to audiences who looked like Sears models.

This was not the mode of Harry Leland Mitchell, who was a lover, rambler, protester, negotiator, and inveterate talker until, toward the end of his long life, finally a writer, too. His autobiography, *Mean Things Happening in This Land* (1979),[41] is both invaluable document and thrilling adventure. For "Mitch," as he was ever known, was a southern Marxist, member of Norman Thomas's Socialist Party, farm-labor union organizer and leader, interracialist, and civil rights activist. In retirement he became an archivist of poor people's memory. Mitch had preserved the papers of the Southern Tenant Farmers' Union, which he had cofounded in eastern Arkansas during the summer of 1934, along with allied collections and a small mountain of invaluable photographs from the 1930s, including some by Dorothea Lang. The originals went to the Southern Historical Collection at Chapel Hill. Microfilmed copies Mitch began to peddle at conventions of professional historians, during the 1970s, while he composed his autobiography. Gradually, then, during a decade and a half, scholars' access to Mitch's "Archives of the Rural Poor," Mitch's own persistent schmoozing with university-based writers of history, and the appearance of *Mean Things* effected profound changes in how the twentieth-century South is perceived. The New Deal's farm program, for one, was a disaster, rewarding the well-off and dispossessing many thousands of tenants and sharecroppers, black and white. And William Alexander Percy's characterizations of humble country people (of both races) become harder to bear. Mitch and his white comrades stand so apart from mean-spirited, dangerous "rednecks" that reconsideration of the tradition is imperative.[42]

Mitch was born in 1906 at Halls, in western Tennessee, hardly five miles from the boyhood home and burial place of the writer Alex Haley. His father was an itinerant sharecropper, barber, and Baptist preacher. Mitch worked much of his first twenty years as a field hand. Unusual for his generation of rural poor, however, Mitch went to high school, fittingly in a town called Moscow (near Memphis), where he encountered a local eccentric who gave him copies of pamphlets by Marx, Eugene Debs, and Upton Sinclair. Mitch was an immediate convert. The other formative event in his life had already oc-

"Redneck" Discourse
79

curred, at the end of 1917, when Mitch was eleven. He took a train to Dyersburg and saw a lynching—actually the burning at-the-stake of a young black man—on the courthouse lawn, before a circuslike crowd of perhaps five hundred. Mitch's closest playmate had been black; he was sickened, and more than half a century later implied that his militant interracialism probably began in Dyersburg.[43]

By the early-1930s Mitch owned a tiny dry-cleaning business across the Mississippi in Tyronza, Arkansas. "Pressing planters' pants while conspiring against them," as Mitch once told me, he brought Clay East, a white neighbor and owner of a gas station, into a radical circle in an unlikely place. The circle included black men and women, some of them Christian ministers, some former Garveyite racial separatists. Together they founded the Southern Tenant Farmers' Union (STFU) which, by about 1938, claimed as many as twenty-five thousand members in five states. Ultimately the STFU was ennervated by attrition (displaced members migrated), and by ideological and racial tensions. For several years, nonetheless, the union staged strikes of cotton pickers, lobbied the federal government for equitable distribution of New Deal subsidies, fought evictions by planters, and most important, created a wonderful interracial movement culture.

During World War II, most of the STFU's leadership and cadres scattered into the military and defense jobs and across the nation. Mitch began an association with the American Federation of Labor that carried him to California to work with migrant farm workers, to Louisiana to help striking strawberry growers and sugar cane cutters, and to Washington. Throughout, Mitch perceived the labor and civil rights movements as inseparable, demonstrating the continuity of Depression-era struggles with the black southern revolt of the 1960s, when Mitch himself confronted the Ku Klux Klan in Louisiana. Later, probably uncomfortable that he, a relatively privileged white man, was to be the old STFU's sole autobiographer, Mitch dedicated his memoir to the redoubtable John L. Handcox. During the 1930s, Handcox was a young black sharecropper and union organizer. Mitch remembered him best, however, as the STFU's troubadour, the composer and lead singer of union songs. One of them Handcox called "There Is Mean Things Happening in This Land," providing Mitch his touching title.

*L*inda Flowers is, I suspect, a largely unnoticed southern autobiographer. This is because she and her family are subsumed within a scholarly monograph devoted to the social pathology of one of the South's economic backwaters, the coastal plain of North Carolina.[44] Flowers is another English professor, a daughter of the subregion who has returned to the old country, to North Carolina Wesleyan College in Rocky Mount, after years away in the North. Her professional speciality is Renaissance literature; she is a Shakespearian, not a southernist. But her return led to an uncomfortable reengagement with eastern Carolina that is both intellectual and emotional. The Ford Foundation sponsored her studies of schooling, which became deeply historical, economic, and personal. The result was an asymmetrical but compelling work called *Throwed Away: Failures of Progress in Eastern North Carolina.*

The main title is a complex expression "peculiar to eastern North Carolina," Flowers explains. It "is pejorative, though often but mildly—sadly—so." Sufferers from the blues or miscreant children might seem "throwed away" for the moment or a day. But so are abandoned cropfields, houses, schools, churches, industrial plants, and unemployed people "throwed away." Flowers insists she is "not labeling people and place in general"—everyone is not ruined—but "rather . . . to make clear a set of historical circumstances—tenantry and its demise, the coming of plants and factories, the altered tenor of public education—the effects of which have been devastating to some people."[45] Flowers's own family are not exactly "throwed away," but irresistibly, they illustrate many of those historical circumstances.

Flowers was born in 1944 at Faison, in Duplin County. Her

grandfather and father were tobacco tenants for an absentee landlord. Flue-cured tobacco was still a quarter-century away from mechanization; so at a time when other tenants were evicted or fleeing to other work, tobacco tenants were relatively secure, themselves hirers of labor in spring and late summer. Linda's mother worked at home, in the house, of course, but also in the fields, and sometimes in tobacco, with neighbors. Faison was itself a bustling, familiar town. Churches and schools were reliable transmitters of cultural stability. Linda's high school class of 1963 was the last of the long age of segregation and, she suggests, of an age of innocent expectation.

In the meantime, Flowers's memory is crowded with familial and local geographical detail. There are ancestors, the landlord who gave Faison its name, inviting little stores, long lines at the cotton gin during picking time, carefree play in tobacco barns, a child's tea set arranged in the dirt under a porch, classmates (including a future astronaut), bosom friends. Flowers also imposes historical understanding upon memory—the details of cotton culture's slide and ruin in the Southeast, the diplomacy of renting farmland, etiquettes of race and labor relations, and powerful intimations of structural change already underway. The new Hamilton-Beach plant contended with landlords and tenants alike for labor, the tenants having less margin to compete. High schools consolidated. Children learned bus routes, preparing them for longer journeys.

Flowers's rendering of all this—and so much more—is no sentimental excursion, although sentiment clearly propels her conflation of family and historical process. Her hardworking parents' last years of farming are almost elegiac. Her observations on machines' efficiencies and enormous costs in human alienation are succinct, subtle, and profound. Flowers is never the preacher, nor are her people saints. Yet in tone, her memoir captures a resignation reminiscent of Old Testament sermons. History has *happened* to mostly good people, who did the best they could. In this important sense, Linda Flowers resembles three fiction writers whom I also admire.

The Countercultural South

The best-known among these is Bobbie Ann Mason. A creature of western Kentucky—Paducah and environs—Mason, too, has been true to her place and folks. (She has recently returned to Kentucky, following a protracted exile in Pennsylvania.) My favorite among her lengthening shelf is *In Country*.[46] This is the coming-of-age story of a seventeen-year-old girl called Sam, set in 1984. Her father was killed in Vietnam before she was born, and she lives with her uncle, Emmett, a zonked-out survivor of the war. Sam smokes dope, drinks whiskey, runs long distances for her health and repose, considers early marriage to a high school basketball star, but loves her ten-year-old VW beetle with the bad transmission, and Bruce Springsteen. She is America, "Generation X-minus," perhaps, the working-class version ignored in essays and movies. Sam shares with Emmett and his lay-about buddies down at McDonald's a lostness derived from the war. This Sam and Emmett redeem, or at least salve, by a pilgrimage to the Wall in Washington, in company with Mamaw, Sam's paternal grandmother. Mamaw's own losses and Sam's uncertain prospects are at least as poignant as the veterans' static gloom.

For Hopewell, Kentucky, the novel's principal setting, is a place of little hope in the 1980s. Always a backwater, anyway, now Hopewell suffers along with the postindustrial world, left behind, throwed away as it were. McDonald's and the Burger Boy offer low-wage employment to youths and some of their elders. Sam and her contemporaries would move away, but meanwhile endure, sedated by popular culture. Mamaw and her husband, Pap, are aged family farmers, typical of a shrinking type, where they survive at all. They are upright, sweet provincials who assumed that had their son lived, he would have taken their place. Vietnam's victims accumulate, long after the killing stopped. Such folk find assurance and comfort where they may. And altogether, Mason's rendering blends the hilarious with ineffable sorrow, leaving readers with a proper sense (I believe) of humans' limited mastery of their lives.

This is the sense, too, of Dorothy Allison's first novel, the acclaimed *Bastard Out of Carolina*.[47] A mounting drama of incestuous child abuse drives the story, but it would be a shame if Allison's book were lumped with the *Oprah/Geraldo*-driven contemporary obsession with this darkest of social pathologies. *Bastard Out of Carolina* is a story of conflicted love that does not trivialize either aspect of the conflict. The heroine of the novel, Anney Boatwright, loves her first daughter, the "bastard" Ruth Anne (called "Bone"); she also loves her new husband, Glen, who becomes as consumed with Bone as with Anney. There can be no untragic resolution for a woman of Anney's intense "hunger for love." Glen, we are to accept, also deserves compassion. This Allison reveals, finally, through Bone, who is the novel's voice and victim, but also deeply the beneficiary of Anney, of her marvelous Aunt Raylene, and other memorable Boatwright kin.

Bastard Out of Carolina takes place in Greenville County, South Carolina, between 1955 and 1962 (when Bone is five to twelve years old)—on the cusp of the age of interstate highways and of the exportation of cotton mill jobs to Asia. The Boatwright clan are what is called white "trash." Anney quit a mill job because the air was bad, became a waitress in a diner (where she met Glen), and then, when Glen could not hold a job, returned to the mill. Other Boatwright women are similarly the mainstays of families. Boatwright men are rather larger than life, more two-dimensional, almost mythical. They work temporarily at construction or what-not, spend most of their time working on cars and trucks, drinking, smoking, shooting at each other for fun, fighting seriously, crashing vehicles into objects stationary and moving, and serving sentences at the county prison farm. They bear a certain resemblance, indeed, to the contemporary Mississippi "rednecks" V. S. Naipaul's informant described: wildly independent, country music fans, mechanical geniuses. Except that Naipaul's expert thought the men "not too sexual. They'd rather drink a bunch of old beer. And hang around with other males and go hunting, fishing."[48] Many of Allison's men are dashing, irresistible to women, and inveterate romantic fools, especially Bone's Uncle Earle. (In the long literary tradition, even William Byrd found "Lubber" men lubricious—this being their only virtue, since the colony needed populating.) The Boatwrights male and female are mostly strong, self-sufficient and resourceful, fiercely loyal to each other, and confident. Glen's appearance in the extended family, however, introduces not only poor Bone's dawning horror but also open class resentment. For Glen's father is a successful businessman, his brothers, professional men. They torture Glen, the embarrassing ne'er-do-well, and snub Anney, Bone, and little sister Reese. Some readers might conclude that the bourgeoisie are responsible for Anney's and Bone's tragedy, because Glen's rage is clearly rooted in his cruel, disloyal middle-class family, a tribe that lacks the Boatwrights'—especially the women's—sense of fate and forgiveness. This seems to me a timelessly appropriate sensibility, but one lost in a consumerist world where "choice" is foolishly extended to philosophy and situational ethics. The Boatwrights know that we are not individually responsible for our fates. They are both orthodox Calvinists and radical political economists.

*C*onstance Pierce is another tragi-humorist who understands this. Pierce spent her first years on a mountain farm in Virginia, then, because her father was a soldier, moved about the world before settling in eastern North Carolina, not far from young Linda Flowers, who is almost the same age as Pierce. There she went to high school, college, and earned her first graduate degree. Ultimately Pierce also became an English professor, but unlike Flowers, she has not returned to live in the South. Her first poetry and fiction reflect her cosmopolitan, international experience—her northern doctoral education, long residences in Latin America and especially Europe, her familiarity with other languages.[49] In fact Pierce, like so many of us, had happily fled the stifling South. Her return, in more recent fiction, may amount in part to the sort of affectionate reconciliation with old places many of us undergo in middle age. If reconciliation it is, however, peace is bitter as well as sweet, layered with irony. Pierce's literary imagination is informed profoundly by her rural and working-class background, her wit (which may be vulgar or subtle), her deep sympathy for men, her impatience with maddening constraints upon women, her respect for all work, and her quiet outrage with merciless political economies.

Consider Vern Pender, for instance, the protagonist of Pierce's story "Memphis."[50] Vern is a truck driver from Kosciusko, Mississippi, making his thirteenth vacation trip to Graceland—all to accommodate Gene, his blimpy nineteen-year-old son "with the mind of a three-year-old." Vern is already disposed toward philosophy—"the more things changed, the more they didn't," he likes to recall; but Gene's gargantuan consumption of "junk," from any sweet drink and fast food to cheap souvenirs and glittery imitations of anything, have driven Vern to apocalyptic cultural criticism. (Gene, who is also addicted to prescription drugs, bears more than passing resemblance to the pathetic late Elvis; and Lucy, Vern's wife, is the match for Elvis's indulgently loving mother.) Vern will carry into Graceland his hunting rifle, appropriately concealed in a guitar case—the story shadows (mocks?) Robert Altman's *Nashville*—he will take hostages at the Presley cemetery, and before the national media, offer his critique of Gene, Elvis, the shopping mall across the highway, of America, his "voice crying in the Wilderness of American life."

Naturally, things go awry. Darkness falls on Graceland, all but two hostages slip away, and there is only a video camera and recorder, no national media. Police snipers wound Vern and carry him off to the hospital, ignominiously. Meanwhile, however, Vern's exchanges with Glendora, a middle-class North Carolinian, and her daughter, who is writing a master's thesis on Elvis as folk hero, convey Vern's (and Pierce's) message well enough. Glendora is embarrassed to be seen at Graceland, preferring, she says, Arlington Cemetery, Gettysburg, and Grant's Tomb. Her daughter's scholarship almost dignifies her trashy Memphis tour, but Glendora will redeem herself, she says, with a visit to the Lorraine Motel memorial to Martin Luther King Jr. Vern's riposte is savage: "She thinks that people who vacation in Arlington Cemetery and Gettysburg's got class, of some kind, and it's true: they do. It's called Trying-to-hang-on-in-the-middle-and-not-slip-to-low-class. But they still like graveyards and big houses, just like the folks that come here. And when they go home from one of those places, they still take some kind of junk with them—postcards, little replicas of big houses, picture books, teeny little gravestones, somebody's autograph."

Vern thought Glendora overly proud of her native state, too, disparaging by implication Mississippi and Tennessee. North Carolina, Glendora expands, is "Home of the Orton Plantation, Tryon Palace, and the North Carolina Symphony. Home of the oldest state university in the nation and major corporations. Prime real estate." Vern interjects, "North Carolina: home of the grand Wizard, the Charlotte Four, the Wilmington Five, the Greensboro Six. . . . It's a graceless state, ma'am. It's just covered up. Sunbelt syndrome. Graceland Crossing shit."[51]

Glendora's daughter, meanwhile, had provided Vern a precis of her brilliant thesis: "Elvis was a poor boy who made good. It's the American Thing, pure and simple." Vern: "Uh-uh. Elvis was a poor boy who went bad, with good reason." And furthermore: "People don't think Elvis is a king or a hero. They think he's a God. When they come here—unless they come to feel superior—they're wanting Grace. They're wanting Deliverance, from themselves as they've been made to be. They want to look at all this stuff that they can't even see is junk, that's how bad they're in need of Deliverance, and they want to be delivered into themselves, as heroes and kings."[52]

Awaking in the hospital three days later, Vern is repentant. He prays, "Dear God in Heaven, I offer up this prayer of thanks that I ain't got blood on my hand. Deliver me from my goddam affliction and restore Your Faithful Servant to normal life. I ain't a bad sort. I just got a wild hair." But something in his conversation with Lucy causes "the thrill of his old vision" to reappear. Fearfully, Vern shuts his eyes, squeezing hard to black out lucidity. Gradually, "from some place, some inner Graceland," Pierce finishes, "he willed the calm he needed . . . for his affliction to pass into the mystery from which it had come."[53] Too bad, one thinks, for Vern is bound for prison, anyway; he was more interesting with his wild hair of lucidity.

The best of Constance Pierce's southern oeuvre is forthcoming or in progress. There are sequential novels, "Queen of Cotton" and "Tollie and Lily," set in a fictional Hope Mills, North Carolina, during the 1940s and 1950s. Janice is the "queen," a mill-town beauty who ran away to New York City during the war and had Tollie, a love child. Returning to a town in short supply of men, she marries Les, who arrives in a symbolic white pickup but is a hapless fellow. The town more so, for by the time Tollie and her friend Lily are teens, in 1959, artificial fibers are driving cotton culture and the textiles business under. (Hope Mills is more ironic than Mason's Hopewell.) Janice represents her generation of working-class women, bright and ambitious but hobbled by circumstances personal and much larger. Tollie and Lily confront their sexuality in an oppressively hypocritical world.

There are also in Pierce's files growing collections of closely related short fiction. The "Flossie Stories," as she calls them, follow a young girl and her family from eastern Kentucky to Detroit during World War II. And "Rust-Belt Stories" treat, in effect, the next generation in the Middle West, some of whom have risen to the middle class. In all, Pierce's characters are flawed but sympathetic, willful but limited (if not whipped) by other agencies. Situations are often hilarious, but Pierce never employs humor to disparage. Her people—like H. L. Mitchell's, Linda Flowers's, Bobbie Ann Mason's, and Dorothy Allison's—do the best they can.

Four of my six exemplars of appropriate "redneck" writing are women—not an anomaly of serendipitous selection, I suspect. Of the two men, I carry but small brief for Crews; and I always thought Mitch (whom I knew for some years before his death in 1990) a very "feminine" man. This because of his patience and receptivity, his gentle, indirect negotiation of dailiness as well as political issues, and the fact that he clearly *liked* women. So whether innate or socialized (I prefer the latter), the qualities of sympathy and toleration seem to be primarily, but not exclusively, of course, women's. There is precedence, as already observed: Ellen Glasgow, after all, was the first important writer to engage ordinary, including poor, southern white folks sympathetically.

Mason, Allison, and Pierce cannot be followed, like Glasgow, by an era of Gothic grotesqueries. This we have with us already. It is widely (and I think truly) said that in our age of official respect for ethnic diversity, enforced more or less by "politically correct" speech, the only remaining fair game for put-down humor is white southerners. (They are not certified as "ethnic.")[54] My solution to the injustice is war—war of the sort once waged by smart-mouthed African-American, Eastern European Jewish, Irish, and Italian kids on big-city streets: the witty counter-insult, aimed now at the middle class, who have enjoyed virtual immunity since the days of Sinclair Lewis. (Lewis was much too serious about his demolition, anyway.) To be "southern," the wit-war against the bourgeoisie should properly be in the narrative form. Constance Pierce has provided an early volley that I recommend.

Her story "In the Garden of the Sunbelt Arts Preserve" mocks her own academic subclass, but especially dilettantish writers freed from real labor by fortunate marriages, and the wealthy who endow retreats for the creatively arty.[55] This retreat must be near Southern Pines. It is surrounded by golf courses and overpopulated with retired professional medicos from Ohio who, with their wives, are mainstays of the "Foundation" that maintains the old estate that houses the artists. Pierce's alter ego, the story's voice, is a writer-in-residence who has risen socially to conceal her own southern backwoods origin. Grateful for the retreat's leisure and amenities, she is nonetheless uncomfortable, discursively ruminous about class.

Toward the end of a languid day, the other artists drink,

dance, and watch a tape of *The Big Chill* (not actually named in the story), in nostalgic rapture with Hollywood's engineering of nostalgic rapture. Pierce's deconstruction of the film is merciless:

A troubled "ensemble" nearing middle-age reassembles after many years for the funeral of a friend. They pack into the bountiful home of their rich and successful host (entrepreneur extraordinaire), dance to the oldies, long for their lost selves, for the happy days at their expensive university, where they had been happily committed to the important causes. They drink wine, confess, dance some more. In the end, everyone is happier and wiser. Most of their problems have been addressed wisely by their genial host, whose hospitality is boundless, whose wisdom is smug and unreflective, but nobody seems to notice. They love their host! He and his wife become Pater and Mater, save the day. . . . The movie was a big hit with everyone, all across the nation. I can't see it. The self-congratulation alone is insufferable. The new entrepreneur as pater, patron, patron saint, and savior of the day is a suspicious idea. It gives me a chill.[56]

So she retreats outside, to the garden's warmth. The ruminator had been startled in the library earlier by the sudden appearance in the window of "the pale country face of a woman, with eyes the color of swamp water." The Foundation had felt obliged, taking over so much territory, to provide "Public Hours" at the retreat. Admission is free, so this poor woman, who is Pierce's alter ego's alter ego, not risen to academic privilege, has come with her little girl. The uncomfortable writer follows, joining the pair on their inspection of the garden's delights. The scene following, which concludes the story, is impossible to summarize briefly, layered as it is with a complexity of symbols—from botany, human social class, and poignant memory.

"In the Garden of the Sunbelt Arts Preserve," woven with subtle humor, unexpected sharp needles left here and there,

is finally much too serious and important literarily to represent my notion of a war of wit on the condescending and
imperial. I have in mind more vulgar narratives—something
like the following nonfiction, a documentary vignette from my
own experience, which I offer without apology to the ghost of
William Alexander Percy.

*I*n June 1988 the Jaycees of the United States held their annual convention in Richmond, Virginia. The president of the
organization, which used to be called the Junior Chamber of
Commerce, welcomed six thousand delegates and their families in the dulcet intonation of the southern piedmont. The Jaycees met in Richmond, the president proclaimed, to celebrate
capitalism; and for the better part of a week, they did. George
Bush and Ted Turner flew in (on separate days) to address
the convention on entrepreneurship, the business climate, and
public policy. The delegates sat segregated by state but locked
arms in their common devotion to private enterprise, booster-
ism, and voluntary community service. There was no discern-
ible sectionalism among the Jaycees, just the friendly rivalry of
cities and states. Only the subject of women provoked so much
as a sectional comparison, and that but briefly on the first day.
The Jaycees had finally admitted females to membership a few
years before, and women comprised thirty-three percent of
the organization nationally. *Thirty* percent of southern chambers were female. So Dixie was a little behind, as usual, but
not by much and probably not for long, promised the drawling
president and numerous southern delegates. Young capitalist
men—and women—could change the world.[57]

Arguably the Jaycees are the symbolic embodiment of
American bourgeois culture. They are realtors and developers, sellers of insurance (among many other things), members of learned professions, and striving occupants of the
lower and middling levels of corporate infrastructures. At
home and in convention, they are self-conscious celebrants of
the entrepreneurial individualism that utterly dominates the

nation's mythology and political rhetoric.[58] Acknowledging all this, and faced with the unhappy circumstance of sharing a midtown hotel with the boisterous delegations of Maine and Pennsylvania, I decided to observe the Jaycees with care. Such study and reflection seemed somehow instrumental to my work in progress, for I was spending my days in Richmond archives among the artifacts of nineteenth-century open-range husbandmen and woodsmen, who were many things but were not bourgeois.

So who were these Jaycees, northern and southern? Who could limn their origins, estimate their virtues, grant them justice? Surely not I. It is said their forebears defied physical law, arising from anonymity gripping their own bootstraps and creating national wealth, suburban conformity, the Methodist church, and the United Way. Conceivably, this is so. But still I studied the delegates. They seemed the most unprepossessing breed on the wide face of an overpopulated planet. Well-fed and dressed in polyester, the men sported red suspenders and styrofoam boaters; the women wore shorts, T-shirts, and more fake boaters. They were self-confident and loud, mistaking euphemism for wit, cleverness at trade for intelligence, and ritual for reverence. They were the sort of people who pray and recite the Pledge of Allegiance in Mariotts and eat pizza, guzzle beer, and play kazoos in the hallways afterward. They were sovereign Americans, our emblems and factotums. It was so horrible it seemed unreal.

Notes

Introduction

1. See especially Elizabeth-Fox Genovese and Eugene D. Genovese, *Fruits of Merchant Capital: Slavery and Bourgeois Property in the Rise and Expansion of Capitalism* (Oxford: Oxford University Press, 1983). On leisure and indiscipline among backcountry whites, see Grady McWhiney, *Cracker Culture: Celtic Ways in the Old South* (Tuscaloosa: University of Alabama Press, 1988), which, although ethnographically wrongheaded, is correct on ordinary white males' culture.

2. See, among other works, Steven Hahn, *The Roots of Southern Populism: Yeoman Farmers and the Transformation of the Georgia Upcountry, 1850–1890* (New York: Oxford University Press, 1983); Edward L. Ayers, *Vengeance and Justice: Crime and Punishment in the Nineteenth Century American South* (New York: Oxford University Press, 1984); David Carlton, *Mill and Town in South Carolina, 1880–1920* (Baton Rouge: Louisiana State University Press, 1982); Ronald D. Eller, *Miners, Millhands, and Mountaineers: The Industrialization of the Appalachian South, 1880–1930* (Knoxville: University of Tennessee Press, 1982); and esp. Edward L. Ayers, *The Promise of the New South: Life After Reconstruction* (New York: Oxford University Press, 1992).

3. See Gavin Wright, *Old South, New South: Revolutions in the Southern Economy Since the Civil War* (New York: Basic, 1986), esp. 4–14, 124, 55, and 198–264; Jack Temple Kirby, *Rural Worlds Lost: The American South, 1920–1960* (Baton Rouge: Louisiana State University Press, 1987); and the works of James C. Cobb, esp. *The Selling of the South: The Southern Crusade for Industrial Development, 1936–1980* (Baton Rouge: Louisiana State University Press, 1982); *Industrialization and Southern Society, 1877–1984* (Lexington: University Press of Kentucky, 1984); "Making Sense of Southern Economic History," *Georgia Historical Quarterly* 71 (Spring 1987): 53–74; and "Beyond Planters

and Industrialists: A New Perspective on the New South," *Journal of Southern History* 54 (February 1988): 45–68.

4. On southern stereotypes in popular culture, see Shields McIlwaine, *The Southern Poor White: From Lubberland to Tobacco Road* (Baton Rouge: Louisiana State University Press, 1939); Sylvia Jenkins Cook, *From Tobacco Road to Route 66: The Southern Poor White in Fiction* (Chapel Hill: University of North Carolina Press, 1976); Donald Bogle, *Toms, Coons, Mulattoes, Mammies, and Bucks: An Interpretive History of Blacks in American Films* (New York: Viking, 1973); Jack Temple Kirby, *Media-Made Dixie: The South in the American Imagination* (Baton Rouge: Louisiana State University Press, 1978); and John Shelton Reed, *Southern Folk, Plain and Fancy: Native White Social Types* (Athens: University of Georgia Press, 1986). Southern female typology is barely examined, and I demur from undertaking here the overdue study of the subject. The third chapter, however, suggests a treatment of working-class white women.

5. Tad Friend, "White Hot Trash!" *New York*, 22 August 1994, 22–31 (first quotation, 28; second, 31).

6. Earl Black and Merle Black, *Politics and Society in the South* (Cambridge: Harvard University Press, 1987), 60–61 (esp. table 3.3, p. 61). The Blacks averaged four presidential election-year polls on the question to arrive at their percentages; thus, all do not quite equal 100.

7. Ibid., e.g., 216–17.

8. Yet most whites of both classes called themselves "conservative." See ibid., 59 (table 3.2).

Chapter 1: Negotiators/Nonnegotiators

1. On Stagolee, see Lawrence W. Levine, *Black Culture and Black Consciousness: Afro-American Folk Thought from Slavery to Freedom* (New York: Oxford University Press, 1977), 413–15; and Dave Marsh, *The Heart of Rock and Soul: The 1001 Greatest Singles Ever Made* (New York: Plume/New American Library, 1989), 161–62.

2. Nathan McCall, *Makes Me Wanna Holler: A Young Black Man in America* (New York: Random House, 1994), parts 1 and 2.

3. See testimony to Southampton Court of Oyer and Terminer, 3 Sept. 1831, in Henry Irving Tragle, ed. and comp., *The Southampton Slave Revolt of 1831: A Compilation of Source Material* (Amherst: University of Massachusetts Press, 1971), 195.

4. McCall, *Makes Me Wanna Holler*, 249–56, 290–99 and passim.

5. See ibid., 244–404 (on penny-loafers, 295–96).

6. I am not alone in this reading: see the review by Adam Hochschild, "A Furious Man," *New York Times Book Review*, 27 February 1994, p. 11–12.

7. The blurb appears on the dust jacket of *Makes Me Wanna Holler*.

8. McCall, *Makes Me Wanna Holler*, 401.

9. E.g., on PBS's *Charley Rose* show, 18 February 1994; ABC-TV's *20/20*, same date; and in an interview on National Public Radio's morning news broadcast, 21 February 1994.

10. On black migration, social disintegration, and Robert Taylor Homes, see Nicholas Lemann, *The Promised Land: The Great Black Migration and How It Changed America* (New York: Random House, 1991), 105–7 and passim.

11. Cornel West, *Race Matters* (1993; New York: Vintage, 1994), 17–31 (quotations, in order, 22–23, 24–27). Emphasis in West's definition of nihilism is deleted here.

12. Eugene D. Genovese, *Roll, Jordan, Roll: The World the Slaves Made* (New York: Pantheon, 1974), 3–25 (quotation, 4). See also Elizabeth Fox-Genovese and Eugene D. Genovese, *Fruits of Merchant Capital: Slavery and Bourgeois Property in the Rise and Expansion of Capitalism* (New York: Oxford University Press, 1983), esp. chapters 1, 2, 7, 9.

13. Genovese, *Roll, Jordan, Roll*, esp. 25–49; and Orlando Patterson, *Slavery and Social Death: A Comparative Study* (Cambridge: Harvard University Press, 1982), esp. 299–333.

14. See, among many sources, Levine, *Black Culture and Black Consciousness*, esp. chapters 1, 2, 5; Gilbert Osofsky, ed., *Puttin' On Ole Massa: The Slave Narratives of Henry Bibb, William Wells Brown, and Solomon Northup* (New York: Harper & Row, 1969); and esp. Henry Louis Gates, Jr., *The Signifying Monkey: A Theory of Afro-American Literary Criticism* (New York: Oxford University Press, 1988). The analogy to parasitism is from Patterson, *Slavery and Social Death*, 334–42.

15. See Willie Lee Rose, *Rehearsal for Reconstruction: The Port Royal Experiment* (1964; New York: Vintage, 1967); and Leon F. Litwack, *Been in the Storm So Long: The Aftermath of Slavery* (New York: Knopf, 1979).

16. See Eric Foner, *Reconstruction: America's Unfinished Revolution, 1863–1877* (New York: Harper & Row, 1988), 396–99 and passim; and esp. Thomas Holt, *Black over White: Negro Political Leadership in South Carolina During Reconstruction* (Urbana: University of Illinois Press, 1977), parts 3 and 4.

17. Foner, *Reconstruction*, 124–75.

18. Ibid., 173–75; Edward L. Ayers, *The Promise of the New South: Life After Reconstruction* (New York: Oxford University Press, 1991), 187–213.

19. Ronald L. F. Davis, *Good and Faithful Labor: From Slavery to Sharecropping in the Natchez District* (Westport, Conn.: Archon, 1982); and Roger L. Ransom and Richard Sutch, *One Kind of Freedom: The Economic Consequences of Emancipation* (Cambridge: Cambridge University Press, 1977), 6–7, 232–36.

20. Among the many authorities on this subject, see C. Vann Woodward, *Origins of the New South, 1877–1913* (Baton Rouge: Louisiana State University Press, 1951), esp. 175–204; and Pete Daniel, *The Shadow of Slavery: Peonage in the South, 1901–1969* (New York: Oxford University Press, 1972).

21. Jack Temple Kirby, *Rural Worlds Lost: The American South, 1920–1960* (Baton Rouge: Louisiana State University Press, 1987), esp. 142–44, 155–56.

22. The best-known, and self-appointed spokesman for twentieth-century paternalism, was William Alexander Percy, *Lanterns on the Levee: Recollections of a Planter's Son* (1941; Baton Rouge: Louisiana State University Press, 1973), esp. 270–84.

23. Kirby, *Rural Worlds Lost*, 133–45 and passim.

24. Theodore Rosengarten, *All God's Dangers: The Life of Nate Shaw* (New York: Knopf, 1974).

25. Ibid., 159 (quotation).

26. Ibid., 511–12 (quotations).

27. Ibid., 312–44, 393–94, 585–87; George B. Tindall, *The Emergence of the New South, 1913–1945* (Baton Rouge: Louisiana State University Press, 1967), 379–80.

28. See Donald H. Grubbs, *Cry from the Cotton: The Southern Tenant Farmers' Union and the New Deal* (Chapel Hill: University of North Carolina Press, 1971); Kirby, *Rural Worlds Lost*, 152–53, 259–71; and H. L. Mitchell, *Mean Things Happening in This Land: The Life and Times of H. L. Mitchell, Cofounder of the Southern Tenant Farmers Union* (Montclair, N.J.: Allanheld, Osmun, 1979), esp. 27–230, 271–301.

29. See, e.g., Lemann, *Promised Land*, 1–58.

30. See Wilson Record, *The Negro and the Communist Party* (1950; New York: Atheneum, 1971), 11–12; and Jacqueline Jones, *The Dispossessed: America's Underclasses from the Civil War to the Present* (New York: Basic, 1992), 143–44.

31. Jones, *Dispossessed,* 259–60; A. Philip Randolph and Chandler Owen, "Our Reason for Being," *The Messenger* (August 1919), 11–12, in August Meier, Elliott Rudwick, and Francis L. Broderick, eds., *Black Protest Thought in the Twentieth Century,* 2d ed. (Indianapolis: Bobbs-Merrill, 1971), 81.

32. Jones, *Dispossessed,* 259 (quotations); and August Meier and Elliott Rudwick, *Black Detroit and the Rise of the UAW* (New York: Oxford University Press, 1979).

33. Jones, *Dispossessed,* 6, 260–61, 269–84.

34. McCall, *Makes Me Wanna Holler,* 170 (quotations).

35. Ibid., 81 (first three quotations), 82 (remaining quotations, emphasis added).

36. See Andrew R. L. Cayton and Peter S. Onuf, *The Midwest and the Nation: Rethinking the History of an American Region* (Bloomington: Indiana University Press, 1990), esp. 84–102.

37. The literature on this subject is large, if sometimes unselfconscious. See, e.g., August Meier, *Negro Thought in America, 1880– 1915: Racial Ideologies in the Age of Booker T. Washington* (Ann Arbor: University of Michigan Press, 1963); and most of the selections in Meier, Rudwick, and Broderick, eds., *Black Protest Thought.*

38. McCall, *Makes Me Wanna Holler,* 292 (first three quotations), 397 (remaining quotations).

39. Ibid., 61 (on "crazy niggers"), 397 (first two quotations).

40. But not without growing impatience. See Ellis Cose, *The Rage of a Privileged Class* (New York: HarperCollins, 1993); and Leonce Gaiter, "The Revolt of the Black Bourgeoisie," *New York Times Magazine,* 26 June 1994, 42–43.

41. See West, *Race Matters;* and among his other works, *The Ethical Dimensions of Marxist Thought* (New York: Monthly Review Press, 1991); and *Prophecy Deliverance! An Afro-American Revolutionary Christianity* (Philadelphia: Westminster Press, 1982).

42. Henry Louis Gates Jr., *Colored People: A Memoir* (New York: Knopf, 1994). The author of this work's dust-jacket summary describes the Gateses as "middle-class," for some reason.

43. See ibid., 8 (on black class uniformity), and 12 (on renting).

44. See ibid., 26, 66, 99, 198 and passim.

Chapter 2: Retro Frontiersmen

1. V. S. Naipaul, *A Turn in the South* (New York: Knopf, 1989), 211.

2. On medieval forests and various Robin Hood legends, see Robert Pogue Harrison, *Forests: The Shadow of Civilization* (Chicago: University of Chicago Press, 1992), 61–102. Sources on southern forest arson are presented in discussion below.

3. On Indians' and colonists' use of fire, see among many other sources, Timothy Silver, *A New Face on the Countryside: Indians, Colonists, and Slaves in South Atlantic Forests, 1500–1800* (Cambridge: Cambridge University Press, 1990), 59–64, 181–82.

4. Readers versed in the volatile and ongoing post–Frederick Jackson Turner historical and geographical literature on frontiers will understand, I hope, that this essay employs the term in the popular "Turnerian" sense understood by V. S. Naipaul and his Jackson informant: that a frontier is an economically undeveloped territory lying to the west of a densely populated, developed area.

5. See Laura Wood Roper, *FLO: A Biography of Frederick Law Olmsted* (Baltimore: Johns Hopkins University Press, 1973), esp. 1–123; and Frederick Law Olmsted, *A Journey in the Seaboard Slave States, with Remarks On Their Economy* (New York: Dix & Edwards, 1856), ix (quotation).

6. Olmsted, *Seaboard Slave States*, 64–68; and Charles Capen McLaughlin, ed., *The Papers of Frederick Law Olmsted* (Baltimore: Johns Hopkins University Press, 1981), 135, 140–43.

7. Olmsted, *Seaboard Slave States*, 64–68.

8. Lewis Cecil Gray, *History of Agriculture in the Southern United States to 1860*, 2 vols. (Washington: Carnegie Institution, 1933), 1: 488–92, presents part of this portraiture, as does Frank Lawrence Owsley, *Plain Folks of the Old South* (Baton Rouge: Louisiana State University Press, 1949); but I elaborate further, in agroecological as well as social terms, in *Poquosin: A Study of Rural Landscape and Society* (Chapel Hill: University of North Carolina Press, 1995). See also Carville Earle, "The Myth of the Southern Soil Miner: Macrohistory, Agricultural Innovation, and Environmental Change," in *The Ends of the Earth: Perspectives on Modern Environmental History*, ed. Donald Worster (Cambridge: Cambridge University Press, 1988), 175–210.

9. See David F. Allmendinger Jr., *Ruffin: Family and Reform in the Old South* (New York: Oxford University Press, 1990), 8–56.

10. Ibid.; and *Incidents of My Life: Edmund Ruffin's Autobiographi-*

cal Essays, ed. David F. Allmendinger Jr. (Charlottesville: University Press of Virginia for Virginia Historical Society, 1990), esp. 167–78, 189–209.

11. On the range and Ruffin's fencing reform, see [Edmund Ruffin?], "The Law of Inclosures," Farmers' Register 2 (November 1834): 345–46; Edmund Ruffin, "The Oppression of the Fence Law, and the Dawn of Relief," Farmers' Register 8 (31 August 1840): 504–5; and Forrest McDonald and Grady McWhiney, "The South from Self-Sufficiency to Peonage: An Interpretation," American Historical Review 85 (December 1980): 1095–1118. On millponds and mills, see Edmund Ruffin, [title illeg.], Farmers' Register 5 (May 1837): 41–43; and Edmund Ruffin, "On the Sources of Malaria, or Autumnal Diseases, in Virginia, and the Means of Remedy and Prevention," Farmers' Register 6 (July 1838): 216–28 (quotation, 217).

12. See William M. Mathew, Edmund Ruffin and the Crisis of Slavery in the Old South: The Failure of Agricultural Reform (Athens: University of Georgia Press, 1988), esp. 195–214; but also (on fencing and millponds) Kirby, Poquosin, chapter 2.

13. See Edward L. Ayers, The Promise of the New South: Life After Reconstruction (New York: Oxford University Press, 1992), 187–213 and passim.

14. See Kirby, Poquosin, chapters 2 and 3; and McDonald and McWhiney, "From Self-Sufficiency to Peonage."

15. See Michael Williams, Americans and Their Forests: A Historical Geography (Cambridge: Cambridge University Press, 1989), esp. 238–88; and William Cronon, Nature's Metropolis: Chicago and the Great West (New York: Norton, 1991), esp. 148–206; Ayers, Promise of the New South, 123–26 and passim.

16. W. Scott Boyce, Economic and Social History of Chowan County, North Carolina, 1880–1915 (1917; New York: AMS Press, 1968), 121–26.

17. Williams, Americans and Their Forests, 229, 242, 265–66, 412–13; James E. Fickle, The New South and the "New Competition": Trade Association Development in the Southern Pine Industry (Urbana: University of Illinois Press for Forest History Society, 1980), 63, 126–27.

18. See Fickle, New South and the "New Competition," 447–48, 481–83; and Elwood R. Maunder, ed., Voices from the South: Recollections of Four Foresters (Santa Cruz: Forest History Society, 1977), 150 and passim.

19. See Joseph Cannon Bailey, Seaman A. Knapp, Schoolmaster of

American Agriculture (New York: Knopf, 1945), 109–243; Roy V. Scott, *The Reluctant Farmer: The Rise of Agricultural Extension to 1914* (Urbana: University of Illinois Press, 1970); and Jack Temple Kirby, *Darkness at the Dawning: Race and Reform in the Progressive South* (Philadelphia: Lippincott, 1972), 131–76.

20. On the bias of county agents, see Scott, *Reluctant Farmer*, 288–313. On the restricted labor market, see Gavin Wright, *Old South/New South: Revolutions in the Southern Economy Since the Civil War* (New York: Basic, 1986), 4–14, 198–264.

21. Jack Temple Kirby, *Rural Worlds Lost: The American South, 1920–1960* (Baton Rouge: Louisiana State University Press, 1987), 45–49.

22. Ibid., 46 (quotation).

23. Ibid., 45–46, 48, 80–100, 195–231.

24. See ibid., 30–32; and Arthur F. Raper, *Preface to Peasantry: A Tale of Two Black Belt Counties* (Chapel Hill: University of North Carolina Press, 1936), 146–48 and passim.

25. Kirby, *Rural Worlds Lost*, 66–73, 140–47 and passim.

26. Ibid., 115–54 and passim.

27. See Donald H. Grubbs, *Cry from the Cotton: The Southern Tenant Farmers' Union and the New Deal* (Chapel Hill: University of North Carolina Press, 1971).

28. Ibid.; H. L. Mitchell, *Mean Things Happening in This Land: The Life and Times of H. L. Mitchell, Cofounder of the Southern Tenant Farmers Union* (Montclair, N.J.: Allanheld, Osmun, 1979), 27–208; and Kirby, *Rural Worlds Lost*, 259–71.

29. Kirby, *Rural Worlds Lost*, esp. 261–71.

30. See references on this subject in the previous chapter.

31. Kirby, *Rural Worlds Lost*, 32–49, 353–55 and passim.

32. Thomas D. Clark, *The Greening of the South: The Recovery of Land and Forests* (Lexington: University Press of Kentucky, 1984).

33. Stephen J. Pyne, *Fire in America: A Cultural History of Wildland and Rural Fire* (Princeton: Princeton University Press, 1982), 71–83, 143–60.

34. Thomas D. Clark, *Three Paths to the Modern South: Education, Agriculture, and Conservation* (Athens: University of Georgia Press, 1965), 87; Williams, *Americans and Their Forests*, 287–88; and Alonzo Thomas Dill, *Chesapeake, Pioneer Papermaker: A History of the Company and Its Community* (Charlottesville: University Press of Virginia, 1968), 1–55.

35. See Kenneth B. Pomeroy, "Can Hardwoods Be Controlled?"

Virginia Forests 4 (March–April 1949): 6–7, 11, 13; and Pyne, *Fire in America,* 112, 118, 172.

36. See Maunder, ed., *Voices from the South,* 150 and passim; Seth G. Hobart, George W. Dean, and Edwin E. Rodger, "The History of the Virginia Division of Forestry, 1914–1981" (bound typescript, Virginia Polytechnic Institute and State University library, 1981), 99; Chris Bolgiano, "From Rags to No. 1: The Pulpwood Market in the 1980s," *American Forests* 93 (January–February 1987): 16–19, 57–60; and Peter Beckstrand, "Deforestation in Disguise: A Tree-Planter's Dilemma," *CoEvolution Quarterly* [no vol.], no. 37 (Spring 1983): 12–17.

37. Will Sarvis, "The Great Anti-Fire Campaign," *American Forests* 99 (June 1993): 33–35.

38. Ibid.; and Ed. Kerr, "Update: Forest Arson in the South," *American Forests* 87 (June 1981): 31.

39. Sarvis, "Great Anti-Fire Campaign," 58 (quotation).

40. Kerr, "Update: Forest Arson," 30 (first quotation); and Deborah Borfitz, "In the South: Arson and Apathy," *American Forests* 92 (January 1986): 57 (second quotation).

41. On periodizing southern forests (i.e., "third growth"), see Neil Sampson, "At Issue: The South's Fourth Forest: Will It Measure Up?" *American Forests* 92 (November–December 1986): 10–11, 54; Bland Simpson, *The Great Dismal: A Carolinian's Swamp Memoir* (Chapel Hill: University of North Carolina Press, 1990), 58 (Jack Camp quotations).

42. Kerr, "Update: Forest Arson," 30–31.

43. Ibid., 34–35.

44. See ibid., forest fire table, 34; and Southern Regional Council, map of " 'Po Country': Poor Households as Percent of Total County Households, 1959," and most recently, "Poor Households as Percent of Total County Households—1989."

45. Borfitz, "Arson and Apathy," 24–25.

46. Ibid., 25; Frances A. Hunt, "Are the National Forests Going to Pot?" *American Forests* 93 (March–April 1987): 37–40; and (on moonshining) Kirby, *Rural Worlds Lost,* 204–14.

Chapter 3: "Redneck" Discourse

1. V. S. Naipaul, *A Turn in the South* (New York: Knopf, 1989), 209–10 (emphasis added).

2. On the timing of mechanization, see, e.g., Jack Temple Kirby, *Rural Worlds Lost: The American South, 1920–1960* (Baton Rouge: Louisiana State University Press, 1987), esp. 51–79, 334–60.

3. Albert D. Kirwan, *Revolt of the Rednecks: Mississippi Politics, 1875–1925* (Lexington: University of Kentucky Press, 1951).

4. C. Vann Woodward, *Tom Watson, Agrarian Rebel* (New York: Macmillan, 1938); C. Vann Woodward, *Origins of the New South, 1877–1913* (Baton Rouge: Louisiana State University Press, 1951); C. Vann Woodward, *The Strange Career of Jim Crow* (New York: Oxford University Press, 1955); W. J. Cash, *The Mind of the South* (New York: Knopf, 1941); Vernon Wharton, *The Negro in Mississippi, 1865–1890* (Chapel Hill: University of North Carolina Press, 1947); V. O. Key, *Southern Politics, in State and Nation* (New York: Knopf, 1949); and George Tindall, *South Carolina Negroes, 1865–1900* (Columbia: University of South Carolina Press, 1952).

5. Kirwan, *Revolt of the Rednecks*, 183.

6. See esp. Key, *Southern Politics*, 664–74.

7. Earl Black and Merle Black, *Politics and Society in the South* (Cambridge: Harvard University Press, 1987), esp. 3–74.

8. They are: Shields McIlwaine, *The Southern Poor White: From Lubberland to Tobacco Road* (Baton Rouge: Louisiana State University Press, 1939); Merrill Maguire Skaggs, *The Folk in Southern Fiction* (Athens: University of Georgia Press, 1972); and Sylvia Jenkins Cook, *From Tobacco Road to Route 66: The Southern Poor White in Fiction* (Chapel Hill: University of North Carolina Press, 1976). The subject is irresistible, however, to all anthologists and surveyors of southern literature; see, e.g., John M. Bradbury, *Renaissance in the South: A Critical History of the Literature, 1920–1960* (Chapel Hill: University of North Carolina Press, 1963).

9. See *William Byrd's Histories of the Dividing Line Betwixt Virginia and North Carolina* (New York: Dover Publications, 1967), 54.

10. See Edmund Ruffin, "Publication of the Byrd Manuscripts," *Farmers' Register* 9 (31 October 1841): 577.

11. A. B. Longstreet, *Georgia Scenes: Characters, Incidents, Etc., in the First Half Century of the Republic* (New York: Sagamore Press, 1957), v, ix (quotations, 43–44).

12. See ibid., v; and William A. Owens, introduction to *The Flush Times of Alabama and Mississippi*, by Joseph G. Baldwin (New York: Sagamore Press, 1957), viii–ix.

13. I am influenced, of course, by Edward Said, *Culture and Imperialism* (New York: Knopf, 1993).

14. In addition to the novels, see E. Stanly Godbold, Jr., *Ellen Glasgow and the Woman Within* (Baton Rouge: Louisiana State University Press, 1972).

15. See Bradbury, *Renaissance in the South*, 75–79; McIlwaine, *Southern Poor White*, 193–99.

16. In addition to Caldwell's novels, see Carl Bode, *The Half-World of American Culture* (Carbondale: Southern Illinois University Press, 1965), 170; Robert Cantwell, ed., *The Humorous Side of Erskine Caldwell* (New York: Duell, Sloan and Pearce, 1951), ix–xxxiii; John K. Maclachlan, "Folk and Culture in the Novels of Erskine Caldwell," *Southern Folklore Quarterly* 9 (1945): 93–101; James Korges, *Erskine Caldwell* (Minneapolis: University of Minnesota Press, 1969); and Erskine Caldwell, *Call It Experience* (New York: Duell, Sloan and Pearce, 1951), esp. 23–25, 102–3, 172.

17. Ellen Glasgow, "Heroes and Monsters," *Saturday Review of Literature* 12 (4 May 1935): 34.

18. Cash, *The Mind of the South* (1941; New York: Vintage, 1960), 387.

19. O'Connor quoted in Robert Coles, *Flannery O'Connor's South* (Baton Rouge: Louisiana State University Press, 1980), xxviii, 154.

20. See Sally Fitzgerald, ed. and comp., *Flannery O'Connor: Collected Works* (New York: Library of America, 1988), 137–53, 263–84.

21. Caldwell's vast popularity and the picture-book episode are recounted in Jack Temple Kirby, *Media-Made Dixie: The South in the American Imagination* (1978; Athens: University of Georgia Press, 1986), 51–59 (quotation, 59); but see also William Stott, *Documentary Expression and Thirties America* (New York: Oxford University Press, 1973), 218–23.

22. Cash, *Mind*, esp. 133–37. See also Bruce Clayton, *W. J. Cash, A Life* (Baton Rouge: Louisiana State University Press, 1991).

23. William Alexander Percy, *Lanterns on the Levee: Recollections of a Planter's Son* (1941; Baton Rouge: Louisiana State University Press, 1973), 153 (quotations). On the election, see Kirwan, *Revolt of the Rednecks*, 212–30.

24. Percy, *Lanterns*, 19–20 (second quotation), 149 (first quotation).

25. See Jay Tolson, *Pilgrim in the Ruins: A Life of Walker Percy* (New York: Simon & Schuster, 1992), 94–96, 107–8 and passim.

Notes to Chapter 3

26. See Louisiana State University Press, *Books for Spring and Summer 1994*, inside front cover; University of Georgia Press, *Books for Spring 1994*, 12–13; and various "Yoknapatawpha" conference announcements and issues of *The Southern Register*, newsletter of the Center for the Study of Southern Culture, University of Mississippi.

27. See Bill C. Malone, *Country Music, U.S.A.* (Austin: University of Texas Press, 1968), 139–44 and passim; Bill C. Malone, *Southern Music/American Music* (Lexington: University Press of Kentucky, 1979); and Melton A. McLaurin and Richard A. Peterson, eds., *You Wrote My Life: Lyrical Themes in Country Music*, Cultural Perspectives on the American South series, vol. 6 (Philadelphia: Gordon and Breach, 1992). I have also summarized problems of identity and ideology in *Media-Made Dixie*, 86–90, 135–36, 153–58.

28. See Kirby, *Media-Made Dixie*, 153–58; Richard A. Peterson, "Class Unconsciousness in Country Music," in McLaurin and Peterson, *You Wrote My Life*, 35–62, esp. 57–58; and Lisa Gubernick and Peter Newcomb, "The Wal-Mart School of Music," *Forbes*, 2 March 1992, 72–76 (including the data that "more people with household incomes of $40,000 or above listen to country music radio than any other format," p. 74).

29. Curtis W. Ellison, "Country and Western Music," in Mary Kupiec Cayton, Elliott Gorn, and Peter W. Williams, eds., *Encyclopedia of American Social History*, 3 vols: (New York: Charles Scribner's Sons, 1993), 1: 1775–85; Curtis W. Ellison, "Social History of Country Music," a long manuscript-in-progress on "restoration," fragments in my possession. MCA executive quoted in Gubernick and Newcomb, "Wal-Mart School," 75.

30. See *Forbes* cover, and Gubernick and Newcomb, "Wal-Mart School," 72, 73, 76 (quotations, in order).

31. Sheila Rule, "The Pop Life: Sophisticated Country Tunes for Down-Home Manhattan," *New York Times*, 28 April 1993, B-3.

32. In addition to the songs, one might see Peterson, "Class Unconsciousness," 57–58, for summary.

33. An interesting essay on the usage of "hillbilly" among Appalachian southerners is Pat Furguson, "No Matter What You Call It," *Mid-Atlantic Country* (February 1994): 88. "Terroni" information from personal observation and the confidence of upper-class Italian acquaintances. On the Meratus, see Anna Lowenhaupt Tsing, *In the Realm of the Diamond Queen: Marginality in an Out-of-the-Way Place* (Princeton: Princeton University Press, 1994); and esp. Clifford

Geertz's essay-review in *New York Review of Books* 41 (7 April 1994): 3–4; and John Kifner, "Through the Serbian Mind's Eye," *New York Times*, 10 April 1994, sec. 4, pp. 1, 5 (quotation, 1).

34. Naipaul, *Turn in the South*, 210 (quotations).

35. Ibid., 58 (quotations).

36. John Shelton Reed, *Southern Folk, Plain and Fancy: Native White Social Types* (Athens: University of Georgia Press, 1986), chap. 5.

37. Courtesy of John Shelton Reed, e-mail, 22 September 1993, in author's possession.

38. John Shelton Reed, "Max Weber's Relatives and Other Distractions: Southerners and Sociology," in *One South: An Ethnic Approach to Regional Culture*, ed. Reed (Baton Rouge: Louisiana State University Press, 1982), 45–57 (quotations, 49–50).

39. Harry Crews, *A Childhood, The Biography of a Place* (1978; New York: Quill, 1983).

40. Ibid., 54 (quotations).

41. H. L. Mitchell, *Mean Things Happening in This Land: The Life and Times of H. L. Mitchell, Cofounder of the Southern Tenant Farmers Union* (Montclair, N.J.; Allanheld, Osmun, 1979).

42. Scholarly works indebted to Mitchell's archive include David Eugene Conrad, *The Forgotten Farmers: The Story of Sharecroppers and the New Deal* (Urbana: University of Illinois, 1965); Donald H. Grubbs, *Cry from the Cotton: The Southern Tenant Farmers' Union and the New Deal* (Chapel Hill: University of North Carolina Press, 1971); Paul E. Mertz, *New Deal Policy and Southern Rural Poverty* (Baton Rouge: Louisiana State University Press, 1978); Pete Daniel, *Breaking the Land: The Transformation of Cotton, Tobacco, and Rice Cultures since 1880* (Urbana: University of Illinois Press, 1985); and Kirby, *Rural Worlds Lost*.

43. See Mitchell, *Mean Things*, 1–3.

44. Linda Flowers, *Throwed Away: Failures of Progress in Eastern North Carolina* (Knoxville: University of Tennessee Press, 1990); and author's interview with Flowers, 15 March 1994, Rocky Mount, North Carolina.

45. Quotations from Flowers, *Throwed Away*, xi.

46. Bobbie Ann Mason, *In Country* (New York: Harper & Row, 1985).

47. Dorothy Allison, *Bastard Out of Carolina* (New York: Penguin, 1992).

48. Naipaul, *Turn in the South*, 208.

49. See esp. Constance Pierce, *Philippe at His Bath, a Poem* (Easthampton, Mass.: Adastra Press, 1983); and Constance Pierce, *When Things Get Back to Normal* (Normal: Illinois State University/Fiction Collective, 1986). Biographical detail from various author's interviews with Pierce, author's colleague, Oxford, Ohio, March 1992–May 1994.

50. Constance Pierce, "Memphis," in *Elvis Rising: Stories on the King*, ed. Kay Sloan and Constance Pierce (New York: Avon, 1993), 156–74.

51. Ibid., 170–71 (quotations).

52. Ibid., 172 (quotations).

53. Ibid., 174 (quotations).

54. See, for instance, "Redneck Jokes on the Rise," *New York Times Magazine*, 4 September 1994, 14.

55. Constance Pierce, "In the Garden of the Sunbelt Arts Preserve," in *An Illuminated History of the Future*, ed. Curtis White (Normal: Illinois State University/Fiction Collective Two, 1989), 73–96.

56. Ibid., 90 (quotation).

57. See the Richmond newspapers, 13–17 June 1988 (e.g., *Times-Dispatch*, 13 June 1988, p. 1). I also heard/watched convention news on television (e.g., WTVR-TV's *News at 6*, 14 June 1988) and observed delegates in the flesh in a midtown hotel I happened to share. See also Booton Herndon's history of the Jaycees, *Young Men Can Change the World* (New York: Pocket Books, 1962).

58. On bourgeois culture's dominance in the contemporary South, see Black and Black, *Politics and Society in the South*, 27–34, 45–46, 60, 194.

Index